On
Failure

Published in 2022 by The School of Life
First published in the USA in 2022
930 High Road, London, N12 9RT

Copyright © The School of Life 2022

Designed by Marcia Mihotich
Typeset by Kerrypress
Printed in Latvia by Livonia

A proportion of this book has appeared online at
www.theschooloflife.com/articles

The School of Life is a resource for helping us understand
ourselves, for improving our relationships, our careers and our
social lives – as well as for helping us find calm and get more
out of our leisure hours. We do this through creating films,
workshops, books, apps and gifts.

www.theschooloflife.com

ISBN 978-1-912891-67-2

10 9 8 7 6 5 4 3 2

On
Failure

The School of Life

Contents

Introduction

This is a book about failing: messing up, disappointing others, letting ourselves down and ruining our lives. It's a book that is intended to be read at desperate moments: when we can't stop crying, when all our hopes have been dashed and when we are too ashamed of ourselves to reach out for help.

First and foremost, this book hopes to act as a friend; one who accompanies us in the darkest hours and proffers one or two helpful remarks that momentarily cheer us up – or at the very least, stop us from feeling so alone. We'll meander from this topic to that and explore failure from many angles, but essentially we'll simply be repeating 'I know, I know ...' in a tone of wholehearted sympathy and boundless compassion.

It matters that the authors of this volume have themselves known huge failure (abandonment, infamy, panic, chaos). This is far from a dry, academic exercise or psychological treatise. It's a letter written by one set of desperate humans to another. It has its origins in despair and in a slow recovery from catastrophe. We'll leave the dispassionate textbooks to others.

Given how much suffering and tragedy there is at large, it's striking how few books seem to have been written to comfort us in our hell. An aura of artistic detachment still surrounds so many of the ones that do exist, as if entertainment and enlightenment were the only priorities and disaster chiefly happens to other people. The books may be *about* divorce, unemployment, disgrace, death, exile, ridicule, opprobrium and mental collapse, they may make us sigh and weep, but it is somehow assumed that the reader will not themselves go through something resembling what has been described on the page. They will watch the central character be jeered and spat at, the heroine flee the country, the hero exchange their family home for a hut – and then check the front door is locked, slip into a warm, clean bed and turn out the light in anticipation of a calm tomorrow.

Of course, the closer we get to true, lived tragedy, the harder it is for words to have any useful impact. What can be said to a person who has just lost their livelihood, who has witnessed a loved one die, who is contemplating professional ruin or who will never be able to set foot in their home town again? The challenge is so large, the psyche so ruined, that they might simply prefer silence, which could honour the disaster better than vain arguments.

But there must be a way in which words can be put to use, even now. There is plenty of time to read during crises: many empty hours in the middle of the night on a cancer ward, in an empty marital bed, in a prison cell before the trial or in a little house after a scandal. This book aspires to be read in lonely hotel rooms and on the platforms of deserted railway stations. Its intended audience are those who bewail their fate, who wish they had never been born, who are going out of their minds with worry and who can barely remember a day when they were last not in agony.

Sometimes, at such moments, we might fall upon the Bible. Copies are often left in the bedside tables of hotels. There is certainly comfort within them; from the ancient cadences, the references to distant tribes, the characters who begat X and Y ... The New Testament can be especially tender; it is – after all – one of the great tragedies of world history and filled with love and hope. The man from Nazareth certainly understood suffering. And yet, for so many of us, the book ultimately doesn't work, because we cannot believe in the beatific solutions being proffered. We are in biblical agony, yet godless. We are Job without even someone to question.

The modern world has not served us well. We have been so busy inventing gadgets to save us time and ease minor frictions, and we are so keen on anticipating a more perfect technological future, that we've overlooked the fact that life continues to provide us all with an endless array of tragic plots, which we cannot even appeal to divine forces to assist us with. This is where this book attempts to fit in. It wants to be the resource that we turn to when everything is as bad as it has ever been.

We'll look at two kinds of engagement with failure over the following pages, in their own ways equally harrowing: what we might call *actual failure* and *imagined failure*. By actual failure, we mean every scenario in which a life is destroyed by our own errors and the swerves of fate: bankruptcy, social ruin, romantic disaster, disgrace ... These are explorations and considerations for those who have been severed from loved ones, those who have been arrested or are waiting to be so, those who are in prison, those who have lost all their money, those who will from now on always be pariahs and will never be able to step into 'polite society' again. We'll then look at imagined failure, for those who are ostensibly untouched but are in agony within, for their hell is in their minds. They are in a prison of their own psychological construction, terrified of failure – not just slightly worried, but unable to sleep, haunted by an apprehension of disaster, mesmerised by spectres of ruin and mockery and brought to the edge of suicide by panic about disgrace and shame.

In both cases, the aim is to find our way towards ideas that will make it possible to go on. We won't deliver happiness, as such, but we are interested in endurance – in managing to point the way to an existence where, despite everything, we can keep going, and where there are even occasional small pleasures. A life in which we will be able to smile again, where there might be a little love and laughter – even if, right now, what beckons is seemingly lifelong lamentation.

It is worth pointing out that this is also, along the way, a book about resilience, because if we can survive failure – if we can find a way through the obstacle course – we will never need to be afraid of very much again. True freedom comes from the knowledge that we can get through the worst that life throws at us. We can fail profoundly and still find things, in a way, bearable.

Oscar Wilde, one of the most famous failures of all time, has much to teach us about ruin. At the beginning of Wilde's sentence for gross indecency in 1895, when he was in Wandsworth Prison, he was desperate for reading matter. He managed to have smuggled in for him a Bible, some Plato, Dante's *Divine Comedy*, St Augustine's *Confessions* and works by Walter Pater and Cardinal Newman. It's an intriguing list, and begs the question of what might help someone in prison who is contemplating the destruction of everything they know, who has lost the right to see their children, who has been spat at on the platform at Clapham Common station and who has received hundreds of letters from the public declaring them the most awful person who ever lived. That is an interesting challenge for any book; it sets the bar at an admirable height.

We're taught so much about how to succeed. All the energy and inventiveness of our time is focused there. No one wishes to speak about the less likely, but far more important, possibility that we will witness the destruction of our careful plans. We need a lot of help with failure; we can't allow it to have its victory over us without trying to fight it off with the most vigorous ideas. We're often taught to be suspicious of self-help, and it's true that it has its vainglorious aspects when applied to the questions of how to flatten one's stomach or make a fortune. But self-help fulfils its true promise when we are being helped to find a way out of despair.

Part I:

Real-world Failure

i.

The Many Types of Failure

One of the many cruel aspects of failure is that when it strikes, it can feel like the most unusual and particular event. 'Why did it happen to me?' we wonder, 'Why have I been singled out?' Our failure looks to us like a monstrous exception in an area of life dominated by success – a quite spectacularly strange and rare affliction. We've not only failed, we are – it appears – almost completely alone in having done so. Everyone else's marriage is stable, even terrific; all around us, there are lovers going out on dates and wedding anniversaries being celebrated. Most people's jobs are continuing without trouble; it's hardly 'normal' to be at a loose end at what should be the height of our career. There's no evidence that the others around us have lost command of their reason. The name of no one else we went to school with produces search results that render ordinary social life impossible. How have other people managed not to mess up as badly as we have? We might be indoors, crying and hitting the walls or biting our hands, but outside, children are going to playgrounds, birds are singing, suited figures are attending purposeful meetings, families are laughing, youngsters are planning fifty years of success, shopkeepers are wishing their customers a good day and there will be parties to attend at the weekend. We feel like freakish, pitiable outcasts in a world of triumph, friendship, ease and contentment.

It is this extremely painful impression that deserves to be corrected at once. Failure may seem like the exception when it is being experienced – when we are in a profound crisis – but let there be no misunderstanding: messing up is what humans do and have been doing since the start of our adventure on the planet. Our own, personal failures stand in a prestigious and quasi-essential lineage. We are not alone; we may even be in the majority.

We don't live through our failures all at once, which is where some of the misapprehension and loneliness comes from, and we don't necessarily do it visibly, which is another reason why we're fooled that everyone else is fine, but taken together, humans are both the masters and forced subjects of failure. There is no family in the land without a serious disaster in their midst. Look at a classroom of twenty sweet 5-year-olds; within half a century, a good third of them will have been scarred by a very sharp knife indeed. It would be possible to tell the story of humanity not – as we usually do – as one of progress and gradual mastery, but as one of repeated distress, unshakeable madness and eternal regret. Almost no life goes to plan and few of us come through unscathed – and it's certainly questionable whether all our beautiful machines and complicated accomplishments have made us one jot less troubled than our animal-skin-clad foraging ancestors.

It's this sombre reality that can make us feel such a sense of relief when we see a painting such as Pieter Bruegel's *The Triumph of Death* (see overleaf). Here is a skeleton army marching over a forlorn landscape, butchering everyone in sight. No one gets away. Kings are breathing their last, lovers are being murdered and funeral pyres are burning in the distance. Corpses are swinging from scaffolds, a horse is dragging a cartload of bodies and massed ranks of soldiers of the armies of death are waiting to join the scene of butchery. This is not a representation of any one particular war zone or scene of horror, but it feels familiar because it is existentially correct, true to some basic facts of our own lives and of all peoples: life is endemically connected with cruelty, ruin and disaster.

This may be a horrific fact to take on board, but it is even more horrific to mistakenly believe that the agony might be ours alone – or that we have been promised anything else. What we are going through only looks rare. Our pain only seems exceptional and aberrant because we are looking at false, wilfully edited – and hence cruelly sentimental – pictures of reality.

Let us consider some of the leading categories of failure that compulsively visit the human animal.

Pieter Bruegel the Elder, *The Triumph of Death*, c. 1562–1563

Romantic failure

Astonishingly, we are still inclined to trust that relationships might somehow be the fun, sweet, exciting and endearing bit of life. Let's be clear: there is no faster route to destroying ourselves than through love and sex. There is no more effective way of turning otherwise sensible and balanced lives into tragedies than through engagement with our romantic and sexual drives.

No wonder people are nervous on first dates – they should be a lot more so (especially if the date goes 'well'). The chances of getting through our sex lives unscathed are negligible. No one properly informs us of the risks. There are no warning signs, extensive training programmes, hazard lights and alarms. We don't employ masked figures to wail and intone when adolescence begins. It's like the mouth of an active volcano left without guard rails. There is nothing like the requisite solemnity or fear. Yet so much predisposes us to fail.

For one, we have a hopelessly fragile understanding of our own minds and needs. We can't grasp what we're after and what we should resist. Sex is in permanent conflict with emotional priorities. It's impossible for us to recognise the ways in which our underlying disturbances affect who we can desire – and what unfortunate and reckless choices we continually make due to the imprint of our childhood psyches. It can take a decade to work out that we have landed on a person exquisitely designed to provoke our worst responses. For a while, we may get away with it. No one gets seriously hurt – there aren't any children, there's no money involved, no one else cares. But our luck will only hold out for so long. Gradually, we assemble the ingredients for our own disaster: a slightly compromised marriage, a somewhat damaged psyche, a handful of children, a sprig of boredom, an ounce of jealousy, maybe an affair, some financial wranglings, a divorce, a judgemental society ... In the end, we don't need to do very much wrong in the romantic field to end up involved in horror.

Workplace failure

For the first two highly influential decades of our lives, we are required to work a lot without ever really needing to ask ourselves any of the bigger questions about what this work means: whether the work is right for us or helps us to make a contribution we welcome or can identify with. We just put our heads down and make our way through the educational obstacle course as best we can. But once we graduate, we are thrown off guard. Without warning, the options become more perilous – even as the silence about how to choose from them grows. We want, naturally, to make a comfortable living, but most of us will feel we have failed if our work doesn't at the same time provide us with a feeling of deep satisfaction and meaning. Too often, we confront a choice: between head and heart, between what we ideally want to do and what it would be sensible to settle for. Immediately, the ingredients for failure start to brew. There are those who overestimate their talents, and end up in middle age, broke and disappointed, envious and angry. There are those who underestimate the pull of authentic ambition, and end up materially comfortable, but dissatisfied, ashamed of their cowardice and longing to make changes they cannot afford. We are strung between the pull of safety on the one hand and of fulfilment on the other, each one with a viable claim on us, neither providing us with enough on its own, and with the world rarely willing to offer us both. We need to be very fortunate not to regret having been either excessively weak-willed or excessively foolhardy.

It doesn't help that we are called upon to make the most important choices without the relevant experience needed and without properly understanding ourselves or the conditions of the job market. With little awareness of the seriousness of what we are doing, we accept a position 'for a year or two', only to find two decades later that this shunted us onto a track that we have never been able to escape. We don't sense doors closing; we don't even know where the doors are. There seem to be few people with the relevant experience and patience to talk to. Instead, we wind up sitting at home on Sunday evenings, quietly panicked about the years passing, sensing that something large is not right about our direction but without the courage or resources to know what to do next.

Even if we have had the good fortune to know what our ideal destiny would be, we need to be very lucky indeed for the economy not to trample on our hopes. In almost every field we might consider, there are far more candidates than there are positions. The world is not waiting for yet another author or psychotherapist, furniture designer or anthropologist. Success requires a rare combination of talent and stubborn grit and relentlessness. We may fail not because we lack vision or talent, but because our hearts are too tender.

There is something structural to our misfortune, too: the capitalist marketplace requires that a good portion of its participants fall by the wayside every year. Weaker companies and participants must be eradicated; obstacles to lower prices and efficiency must be removed. Progress demands culls. Customers can only be satisfied if the weaker producers are identified, exposed and winnowed out. The anxiety of our age isn't simply an unfortunate aberration: it is the leading emotion that should logically accompany us into the office.

Further risks abound in the dynamics between workers. There are bullying managers, uncooperative colleagues, undermining subordinates. There is jealousy, backbiting, gossip and persecution. The very quality that we need in our work – ambition – may be what alienates us from other, more lackadaisical workers who won't lose an opportunity to bring us down when they can. The workforce pyramid has very steep sides and the tumbles are brutal and terminal. We will need an implausible degree of luck not to be stabbed in the back, or at least roughed up in the corridors of power.

Reputational failure

Until it is under threat, it is easy to overlook what 'reputation' is or how desperately it matters. Reputation is made up of all the material that people who hardly know us resort to when judging us. It is the repository of all the random, semiconscious associations, prejudices and scarcely examined ideas that surround our names. The material may be inaccurate and casually compiled, but reputation still ends up determining the gospel truth about who we are for people who never have, and never will, give us an honest minute's thought – that is, for almost everyone in the world. The other thing to note about reputation: it cannot be cleansed once it has been sullied.

For a long time in our lives, most of us lack a reputation of any kind. Our name is simply a blank. No one knows whether they should be pleased or appalled to meet us; the internet is silent about our identities. This is a momentous freedom – though it is rarely appreciated as such. Then, because of some superhuman moves on our part (unceasing efforts at work, remorseless networking, desperate attempts to generate publicity), we may start to develop a 'good' reputation. Positive associations begin to hover around our names; strangers may want to meet us. Our social circle becomes filled with people who like us chiefly because they are under the impression that other people like us.

Until one day we make a mistake – perhaps not a very large one, all things considered. We sleep with the wrong person, we send the wrong email, we lose our temper in the wrong place, we say the wrong thing online – and our reputation, carefully built up over three decades, falls apart in two hours. Like death (which it in many ways resembles), reputational extinction can happen in an instant. There are articles in the newspaper, rumours about us at parties – there may even be jeers in the street. Legions of people we didn't even realise existed but who turn out to have been deeply offended by our success now gang up to accuse us of crimes way beyond those we actually committed. We are expelled from the group and sent into status exile.

We want – and may even begin – to protest. We try to put people right. Maybe we send letters pointing out that they have not judged us correctly; that they have got a few facts wrong here and there. We patiently try to explain that they haven't fully grasped the way things look through our eyes. We might launch a court case in a bullish attempt to persuade them of another side to the story – or we might make a grovelling apology, give some money to a good cause, and hope for a second chance.

But we will soon realise that our efforts are entirely in vain. People aren't getting us wrong for sensible reasons. They are generally doing it on purpose, to appease some historic sense of grievance, to assuage the pain of having themselves been overlooked for too long or to have a bit of fun because their own lives are filled with boredom, suffering and humiliation. Or they may hold on to the prevailing ideas about us because they can't be bothered to do anything else; it's just easier. They probably never thought seriously about us until now – and they're not, in the middle of a scandal or a sacking, about to start to reflect deeply on our true character and the injustices of fate. They believed public opinion when we were supposedly marvellous, and they are happy to continue blithely to believe in it now that we are apparently unspeakable. It saves time.

Reputation is not something that can ever be 'repaired' because it is never properly built; it is merely a temporary assembly of wind and twigs. Yet public shaming is about as serious a wound as anyone can suffer. We are social creatures, hard-wired to care immeasurably about what others think of us; our antennae are perfectly attuned to notice how we are being perceived and when we have fallen foul of the community. We can't help but be pained that – however complex and mitigating our true story is – we are condemned, for the rest of our lives, to be known only as 'the criminal', 'the weirdo', 'the loser' or 'the pervert'.

It can feel like nothing we could ever do will be able to correct the mark on our names; we will never be able to reach into the minds of those who disparage us and alter the story that is unthinkingly summoned up whenever we are mentioned. A broken reputation forces us to do nothing less than give up on our relationship with most of the human race; it takes some practice, to say the least.

Parental failure

We dream of close and tender bonds with our closest family members, but without envisaging the consequences, there are certain things we do that can – seemingly irreparably – alienate us from those we love most.

The pain of this alienation can be especially acute with our own children. Despite our good intentions, we may end up behaving in ways that earn us their permanent opprobrium. Perhaps we have an affair or divorce their mother or father; maybe we take a job in another city or force them to relocate to another country. Or, at a time when they were especially vulnerable, we may be visited by problems we cannot control and that we regret every day of our lives: heavy drinking or addiction to drugs, depression or anxiety, being manic or paranoid. Alternatively, we might be beholden to a rigid or naïve theory of parenting or politics. Or more broadly, something might hold us back from expressing the love and care we feel deep down.

Sometimes, there is no way back from our errors. Despite every attempt to apologise, we are told that we are not welcome. We understand; we don't hold it against them. We know that it's not the job of a child to dig deeply into the mind of their parent or to extend empathy towards someone who should always have been there for them in uncomplicated ways. They had a right to expect regularity, predictability and kindness. They never signed up to rages, a scandal all their friends could read about online or a new family they were expected to go on holiday with. No wonder they want to keep their distance.

Now, every time we see a young child playing happily with a parent in the park, we don't just see a scene of innocence and kindness, we receive another reminder of our ineptness and selfishness. We know in no uncertain terms that we are monsters, whose errors have severed us from those it was our simple and ultimate duty to care for properly.

Historic failure

There is a category of failure that has a specifically historical dimension to it. This error is one that might not have been classed as such at one time, but that grows fateful because of a change in the wider political, economic or social context we inhabit. If the times hadn't changed, we might have been safe, but, perhaps without much warning, history moves sharply and we end up on the wrong side of it. Victims of such historic failure might be aristocrats with a castle and ancestral lands before the French Revolution or industrialists with factories in the Caucasus before the Russian Revolution; they might have been those associated with the South Vietnamese government after the fall of Saigon or doctors with Western classics on their bookshelves in Beijing during the Cultural Revolution.

What was once a grey area can become – very suddenly – extremely black. Those with a slightly adventurous sex life find themselves in a time when moral panic is setting in, or someone who hasn't written down all their business expenses is caught short just as the firm decides to enforce its policies more strictly. In situations like these, we know that our 'crime' would once have been waved through – or not registered as an infraction in the first place. For centuries, our forebears would have done exactly as we did. They might well have had servants and a castle, had threesomes, read books by intellectuals or had long lunches at the company's expense – but what they could get away with is able – due to a riptide of history – to ruin our lives.

Every shift of history seems surprising when it happens. We dwell on continuities, but it would be wiser to focus instead on how often history has swerved – and dare to wonder about the areas in which we remain exposed to abrupt shifts in morality and judgement. That may, however, be too optimistic, for it's in the nature of truly dangerous historical zigzags that no one could possibly have predicted them. Instead, perhaps we should simply be soberly aware of the degree to which the 'common sense' or 'normal' behaviour of today could be the grounds for ostracism or jail tomorrow.

Mental health failure

For most of our lives, if we are lucky, our minds do roughly what we want them to. They come alive and fall asleep as we command; they go in the direction we steer them towards. They are quiet when we need to unwind, they are unimaginative when we need to concentrate and they stop repeating ideas when we have heard them sufficiently often.

Until – for some of us – our minds become our enemies. We lie in bed in the early hours and beg them to switch off, but still they continue to buzz and whirr, throwing out random worries and projects and visions as the hours turn from two to three to four – and all chances of a productive day ahead recede. Sometimes our minds get stuck on a particular loop of anxiety: they panic again and again about what might happen during a speech or a meeting, a shopping trip or dinner with a friend. Their ringing gets so loud, their worries so catastrophic, that we have to withdraw from an active life. We reassure them as best we can and still they insist on hysteria. The most minor challenges grow unbearable. We fear that everything is about to come to an end, we see terror everywhere, we have to check and recheck every point of concern – and yet the counsel and wisdom we take in can never stick. Or, afflicted in a different way, we might grow sad and heavy for reasons that our minds refuse to yield: we don't quite know what is unbearable, only that it is so, and that we are wretched and undeserving, and that nothing we do can be good enough – that we would be better off dead.

Few among us who have avoided such torments can take them seriously; they so easily seem like malingering – or pure hallucination.

Those who mention them must be exaggerating. But the sad reality is that our minds are no less prone to malfunctioning than other organs of our bodies, and in no less dreadful ways. They can be instruments of torture. When our minds break down, we find ourselves unable to work, go out in public, approach any challenge with confidence, act as a responsible parent or build new relationships. We live in paranoia about disgrace and shame – we don't trust ourselves not to say something shocking or to harm ourselves or someone we care for. We fail in these instances not because of anything that has happened in the world, but because the minds through which we perceive it have turned against us.

* * *

Ultimately, we are prone to failure because we are tragic animals; creatures whose constitution is inherently unsuited to the complicated tasks thrown up by our long and multifaceted lives. We fail in our ability to read the world with the perspicacity and intelligence required. We don't notice until it is much too late where we have missed clues, where we have been hasty or arrogant, where we have been incautious or conceited. Our minds are not powerful enough, and not well-trained enough, to take on board all the lessons we would need to stay cautious and safe across all the demands we face. We blunder into scenarios assuming we know how to handle them. We worry too much in some areas and not nearly enough in others. We celebrate too soon. We grow proud of ourselves and dare to assume that we know how to live – hubristically believing that we are not at the mercy of what we might as well call – with zero religious intent – the gods. And all the while, our lives dangle on a thread, vulnerable to governments, religions, ideologies, businesses, families and our own fragile neurochemistry.

In the 4th century, the Christian scholar and monk Evagrius the Solitary – who spent most of his life in a hut in the Egyptian desert – defined seven 'evil tendencies' that needed to be overcome in order to lead a godly life. From his list emerged medieval Christendom's resonant concept of the seven deadly sins: lust, pride, greed, wrath, envy, gluttony and sloth. We can imagine these operating beneath most of our disasters – of all the kinds listed above – even today. Christian writers put this dilemma grandly and poetically: we sin not by chance, but because we are the descendants of sinners; all of us are tainted by Adam and Eve's 'original sin' (what St Augustine termed *peccatum originale*). It isn't in our power to insulate ourselves wholly from the worst sides of our nature – man is a faultily designed, congenitally sinning animal.

We may try to be sexually sensible, for example, but the temptations are many and often unheralded. All that tragedy requires is a frustrated marriage and a night away. The ingredients that might have made for banter, an indulgent smile and an unremarkable acknowledgement of appetite when we were single can concoct – once there are legal strictures in place – combustible material for a scandal from which no recovery is possible. We need only have a slightly too intense desire to hold and to be held, to caress, to touch, to lay a hand – and we are doomed. The tripwires are everywhere, artfully hidden: across barriers of age, workplace regulations and internet addresses.

We don't notice ourselves wanting far too much: admiration, money, acclaim. It happens – as it tends to with sins – slowly and imperceptibly. But the more it grips us, the more we lose our ability to spot our errors. We cut corners, make unnecessary enemies and are impatient and careless – we gradually tie the noose around our own necks.

When we are proud, we stop noticing the ways in which we humiliate others; we forget to regularly remind ourselves of how flawed and absurd we are. We start to take ourselves very seriously – and we build up a store of anger in those around us. Every success we chalk up has quietly hurt someone else, and for a long time, they can't protest, because we can dominate and crush them with our power. But we have enemies, there is blood in the water – and when we make a mistake, they will be ready to turn it into an irreparable wound.

We might not think of ourselves as 'lazy', either, but the word doesn't have to be restricted to those who sleep in past midday and don't do the housework. There are deeper kinds of laziness: the intellectual laziness that stops us from examining our own natures; the moral laziness that stops us exhibiting kindness; the professional laziness that prevents us from seeing that we are engaged in ultimately noxious pursuits that are harming those around us.

It sounds old-fashioned to warn anyone of such sins – the word even sounds a little charming or comedic. But sins are nothing of the sort: they are the broken paving stones on which we can trip and shatter our lives. The point isn't really to warn at all – it's too late for that. Simply, to recognise these pitfalls is to provide a little perspective to the reasons why we fail. We should remember that our errors take their place within a more than 2,000-year history of messing up.

To speak in more psychological language, our brains are cognitively, congenitally flawed. They don't give us the information necessary to succeed in our goals – we don't have the right dials on our instrument panel and the warning lights largely don't function. It is appallingly easy to ruin, or at least heavily dent, our lives – and as no one really tells us how not to, most of us at some point will. We should not – on top of it all – ever feel alone with our catastrophes.

ii.

Should I Kill Myself?

The question sounds so shocking that even in the depths of misery we are rarely inclined to address it head on – not least because we are given every encouragement by respectable societal voices to chase it aggressively out of our minds. It can seem as if only the severely unwell would ever seriously contemplate, let alone carry out, such a desperate act.

However, we do ourselves and our lives a serious injustice through evasiveness. We should accept suicide as the real possibility it is – or else it will return as a compulsion in moments of particular despair. The question of existing or not existing deserves dignified and slow examination. People will turn to suicide whether or not the matter is taboo; there can be no risk of incitement through discussion alone, but at least when we have the courage to examine the act rationally, we can develop a better handle on the central intellectual arguments for remaining on the side of life – rather than aligning with it only out of shame, habit, convention or cowardice. A good life requires that we wrestle sincerely with the possibility that we might end it prematurely. Living should be a choice, not a command – and, especially in the wake of serious failure, we need to choose with our eyes open. If we are properly to respect life, we should never be squeamish about dallying for a while – a long and thoughtful while – with the notion that we do not have to be here.

To liberate our thinking, we might start by looking back to the Stoic thinkers of ancient Greece and Rome, among them Seneca, Marcus Aurelius, Zeno of Citium and Cleanthes. In different ways, these philosophers put forward the view that choosing our own end could be a realistic possibility that a self-possessed and intelligent person might opt for after a great deal of reflection, not just a momentary aberration or evidence of mental illness. Exceptionally in the history of the West, the Stoics held that there was nothing inherently shocking or forbidden about ending one's own life. It was, in their eyes, the birthright of every noble and free spirit to choose how long they wished to be here.

For the Stoics, contentment – or as they put it in Latin, *dignitas* – must be founded on a life in which our bodies and minds leave us free of terrible pain, in which outer circumstances do not continually humiliate us and in which mistakes or 'tragic errors' (the Stoics were keen observers of Greek tragedy) do not bring eternal opprobrium and shame upon us.

The Stoics knew we were in danger, however. Our capacity to ensure a pain-free life endowed with dignitas is vulnerable to many forces not wholly within our command: we have little say in the condition of our bodies and brains, the minds of others can quickly fill with unbudgeable prejudices about us and we have passions and tendencies to foolishness that mean we may well unwittingly do something that falls foul of our community's moral code. The term that the Stoics used to capture this vast, uncontrollable inner and outer terrain was 'fortune'. And, as they insisted, key elements of what we require to lead a decent life lie in the realm of fickle and cruel fortune.

The essential objective of Stoic philosophy is to help us reach a position where we are not held hostage or intimidated by fortune's possible whims and vagaries. When we worry, it is common to be told that our dreadful fear won't turn into a reality. But what if it does? We might, in the dark hours, throw out a comment to ourselves that, as soon as we've uttered it, sounds both completely alien and very soothing: 'If things were to get really bad, truly bad – more than I would want to bear – it wouldn't have to go on forever.'

This middle-of-the-night thought is also likely to sound grotesque, outlawed and embarrassing, because we are all – even atheists – the heirs of 2,000 years of emphasis on the sanctity of every life, and of a faith in a benevolent God who assures each one of us of His love right now and His peace in eternity. But the Stoics made it their starting point. Consider this letter Seneca wrote to a friend, sometime around AD 60:

The wise man will live as long as he ought, *not as long as he* can ... *He always reflects concerning the quality, and not the quantity, of his life. As soon as there are numerous events in his life that give him trouble and disturb his peace of mind, he sets himself free. And this privilege is his, not only when the crisis is upon him, but as soon as Fortune seems to be maltreating him; then he looks about carefully and sees whether he ought, or ought not, to end his life on that account. He holds that it makes no difference to him whether his taking-off be natural or self-inflicted, whether it comes later or earlier. He does not regard it with fear, as if it were a great loss; for no man can lose very much when but a driblet remains. It is not a question of dying earlier or later, but of dying well or ill. And dying well means escape from the danger of living ill.*

Seneca was not advocating random or thoughtless exits; he was attempting to give us more courage in the face of anxiety by reminding us that it is always within our power, when we have genuinely tried everything and rationally had enough, to choose a noble path out of our troubles. He was seeking to strip willed death of its associations with pathology and to render it instead an option that the wise always know is there as a backstop. It doesn't need to be a grim spectre, either; the Stoics emphasised that death could be a moment to celebrate what had gone well in a life, to thank friends and to appreciate the beautiful and good sides of the world. The idea was to see death as a door through which we knew we had the right and the capacity to walk when it felt necessary. Seneca continued:

You can find men who have gone so far as to profess wisdom and yet maintain that one should not offer violence to one's own life, and hold it accursed for a man to be the means of his own destruction; we should wait, say they, for the end decreed by nature. But one who says this does not see that he is shutting off the path to freedom. The best thing which eternal law ever ordained was that it allowed to us one entrance into life, but many exits. Must I await the cruelty either of disease or of man, when I can depart through the midst of torture, and shake off my troubles? This is the one reason why we cannot complain of life; it keeps no one against his will. Humanity is well situated, because no man is unhappy except by his own fault. Live, if you so desire; if not, you may return to the place whence you came ... If you would pierce your heart, a gaping wound is not necessary – a lancet will open the way to that great freedom, and tranquillity can be purchased at the cost of a pin-prick.

These ideas sound so alien to us because of the long Christian past that succeeded pagan philosophy – and that deemed suicide a sin greater than murder and a direct offence against God, because it involved killing not only the body but also the soul. Many of us continue to hold on to the Christian views of the end of life even while we don't actually believe in their underlying rationale – and indeed, when we are far closer to the pagans in our pitiless and harsh exposure to fortune. That is precisely why, in order to cope with the anxieties fortune causes us, we should permit ourselves to learn more about a stiffer, franker philosophy than our own. Some of the Stoic philosophers were among the most intelligent, kindly, wise and gentle people who have ever lived. However strange and unfamiliar some of their views may sound, we would do well to extend sympathy to why they held them – and what relief they would have found in them on their most challenging days.

That said, our claim is that there remain three central reasons why suicide is not – after all – to be advised. We can list them systematically.

Firstly: Others

The most common emotion that drives us to think of ending our lives after failure is that we have 'nothing left to live for'. As we contemplate the ruin of our career, the disapproval of friends, the mess of our marriage or the degeneration of our body, we conclude (often very understandably) that there are no plausible reasons to endure. It is at this point that we should try to call to mind something that, especially in these circumstances, can be very hard to hold on to: that there are others – many others – who are relying on us to keep living so that they can remain sane and safe, or indeed themselves continue to live. We may not be able to see these people, and if we do meet them, they may not tell us of their reliance, but the reality is that, were we to take our own life, they would find it more or less impossible ever to return to normality. They would forever take our death as an indictment against them: they would feel that they had not been able to help us as they desperately wished – and they would imagine that our death was a sign that they had not mattered enough to us and that they were therefore neither sufficiently loveable nor adequately worthy. These assumptions might not be remotely true, but it is almost certain that the people who love us would take them to be so in the days, years and decades after our demise. For a select few, our death will be something they simply never get over, and they will feel permanently abandoned. We may not see these people very much, and they may well have been angry or disappointed with us when we last encountered them, but the underlying truth is that their sanity depends on our restraint. There are probably half a dozen or so people on this list directly known to us, and another handful offstage that we might not remember too well, or never even have met, but in whose minds we are nevertheless a potent force (the brother of a friend, perhaps, or a parent of someone we were at school with). And needless to say, on this list are likely the most significant figures of all: our own parents, partners or children – whose existence must be an incontestable, non-negotiable, incontrovertible call to keep going, whatever personal horrors we are travelling through.

When we are muffled by despair and loss, it can seem implausible that someone as wretched as us could ever matter to another human – matter critically – but we do. Immensely. Certain people in our lives right now would quite literally never be able to digest what we are thinking of doing. No day would ever be free of the shadow thrown over them by this incident. People who take their own lives are very seldom trying to deliver an insult to anyone else, they are not trying to tell their children they don't love them or their friends that they don't matter, but this is how – despite every precaution – the act is likely to feel. Furthermore, the consequences of our death will ripple in unpredictable ways through society. When one member of the tribe decides the game isn't worth it, others – ostensibly unrelated – may also despair. The news of our end, in a few lines in the local paper, may be the final encouragement needed for someone else to despair fully of their circumstances. Suicide is catching; it weakens all of our resolve to keep going.

We are evidently not offending God or the angels by taking our own life, but we are doing something far more tangible: we are causing devastating problems for the people around us.

This could feel like a dour and nihilistic philosophy: are we meant to keep going just to avoid burdening others? Is living just a socially mandated chore? It might sound dispiriting, but this idea contains a fortifying, and even releasing, message. We may indeed have nothing directly and personally left to live for, but we possess something far more important to justify our existence: the lives and happiness of other people. Living may not be our wish, but it can be something more robust: our duty.

When in despair, let us remind ourselves that we need to continue for the sake of someone else. We can go on in the knowledge that there is meaning in others' lives – even when we can no longer (at least right now) see it in our own.

Secondly: We cannot predict the future

It's a seldom-mentioned detail that to kill oneself requires a great deal of certainty. It may not seem as though the taking of one's own life would call for intellectual self-confidence or faith in one's powers of forecasting, but it implicitly does. As we prepare the tool to end ourselves forever, it is necessary that we be filled with the conviction that we will always hate ourselves, that nothing about our circumstances can ever change and that the world will never shift in any way towards something more manageable and easier to bear. To kill oneself is to claim to know the future.

However, we should have enough experience of our minds to realise that they have not been endowed with any such infinite power. We can't even foresee how things will turn out over a day – for ourselves or for the world – let alone over three or four decades. There are so many moments in all of our lives when, at 5 o'clock in the afternoon, we feel revolted by ourselves and our chances, only for our spirits to shift and, by 8 p.m., to have turned the corner. We are creatures who don't notice how volatile and temperamental we are. Our moods have a terrible habit of not identifying themselves as such; they claim to represent settled, robust positions when in fact they are merely clusters of temporary associations floating on a complex stream of chemicals.

The tragedy of suicide is that the act allows us one, and only one, mood to determine our entire future. It is therefore profoundly unfair to the many alternative or latent versions of who we are – the sweet self, the curious self, the loving self; unfair to all our selves to be murdered by the present, despairing incarnation of us that is right now dominating the control room of our minds.

As well as our changeable moods and emotions, we should be equally sceptical about the fixity of the world. Certain unpredictable swerves of fate may have brought us to thoughts of suicide: the swerve that created the revolution, the sexual panic, the economic crash, the request for a divorce ... Something major that we hadn't ever thought possible might tip our lives into horror; a dreadful rare event that strips everything of meaning. But in our shock, we cease to notice an element of hope. If fate has swerved into disaster, it might well – with equal unpredictability and suddenness – swerve back into something more bearable. We might not be able to see how the revolution could ever end, how the moral panic might be wound back, how the economy could pick up or how a new lover might enter our lives – but our inability to see a line between our current situation and a bearable future doesn't mean that there won't eventually be one. We could be surprised by hope just as much as we have been surprised by horror.

There is something hubristic and poignant about a claim to know how we will feel and what the world will be like over an extended period that we are in fact stripping ourselves of our ability to witness. Christians once determined that the problem of suicide lay in what they termed 'despair': a loss of hope in the possibility of an intervention from God. But we don't have to rely on miracles in order to hold on to the idea that the circumstances which brought us to our present anguish might over time cede to more benevolent forces. Hopeful things are as likely to happen as unhopeful ones:

history might alter, new inventions and ideas could solve old forms of suffering and love might arrive without warning.

We don't control existence; we should surely have learnt this by now. We can't tell what might unfold. Though we may have experienced the negative side of fate, we shouldn't deny ourselves the chance to live through its possible positives. We don't have to know quite what good thing might happen (we're almost certainly too tired and too sad to do that anyway); only that it might do so.

Thirdly: The power of the imagination

One way to frame the issue is to suggest that, very often, people kill themselves because of a failure in their powers of imagination. They simply cannot picture a better life than the agonised one they currently have; they lose the ability to conjure up images of a more bearable way to be.

This suggests the importance of giving the imagination every encouragement it needs to do its life-sustaining work – and of trying to understand its workings and optimal inputs. By imagination, what we really mean is the power to summon up alternatives. When we are suicidal, it is not possible to imagine finding another job or retraining or shifting profession. We can't imagine not minding about the gossip being spread about us or finding another partner and letting ourselves trust someone again. We can't imagine getting by in a wheelchair, living on a very modest budget or relocating to another country.

It is therefore key to assert a theoretical truth from the outset: with sufficient imagination, almost any problem can be worked around. There are substitutes for most of what we have lost; not ideal replacements, but viable ones. If one door has closed, the imagination can, in time, find another. Every life can be rendered bearable, however unpromising the initial ingredients. If 200 doors have closed, there will be a door number 201 to locate somewhere. If plan A has failed, we can eventually pull together a plan B or C ... or Z. There are an infinite number of ways to lead a life – and it is simply part of our illness that we cannot, as yet, see beyond the one way of life that we loved and have lost. Like a grief-stricken, abandoned lover, we can't picture that there are alternative candidates; but just as we might meet someone new, so can we determine new ways to live.

There are other cities we can go to and completely new kinds of work we can try. There are lovers who have a completely different approach to intimacy from those we have known to date. We are grown-ups – that is, people with choices. We are not the small children we once were who had to depend on their parents for everything and were imprisoned by narrow circumstances. We can build ourselves a small hut on the edge of the desert if we want to. We can work as a carer or retrain as a psychotherapist, find employment in a prison or in a hospice. We can help staff a suicide line (we have a lot of experience in the field already) or volunteer in an emergency shelter. We can change our names. If we're feeling shy and defeated, we don't have to go out and see anyone ever again. We can live by ourselves, mind our own business, read the classics and tend to our garden. We can have a breakdown and then recover; a lot of people do. Should the mood take us, we can throw ourselves into learning a new skill or take a university degree in Sanskrit by correspondence course. We can find the love we need; we only require two friends, or even just one, to get by. Many people might be cruel, but a few are infinitely compassionate and kind and we can go out and find them and not let them go. We could make a new circle of friends among recently released convicts (they tend to be very bright and very free of social snobbery). We could go to a monastery or a nunnery or look up a few old and trusted friends and suggest living together in an unconventional, small and supportive commune. We can rid ourselves of the toxic values we grew up with and become – in the best way – outcasts and eccentrics.

We don't have to stick to the script we thought we'd be following all our lives. We might have wanted to do so, but we are profoundly flexible creatures. When we arrived on the Earth, our mental wiring was loose enough that we could have developed into excellent foragers in the Kalahari Desert, Latin scholars in a university or accountants in the logistics industry. Our biology is elastic. We may have lost a little of that primordial flexibility, and it might no longer be so easy to pick up new languages or physical skills, but we remain eminently equipped to acquire new tricks. Other people – noble and interesting people – have been here before us. There have been exiled Russian princes who have learnt how to become tennis teachers; émigré South Vietnamese army generals who have started kindergartens; divorcees who have remarried in their eighties; shamed executives who have opened flourishing corner shops.

In order to increase our chances of survival, we need to feed and massage our imaginations; we need to provide them with examples of alternative narratives, so that they can grow more skilled at throwing out plan Bs when fate commands. We must give them books to read about countesses who found happiness with manual workers, potentates who learnt to get by on modest pensions and cities that were rebuilt after being burnt to the ground. Whatever way we happen to be living, we should constantly force ourselves to picture different, more arduous, but still bearable ways to be, imagining ourselves as pilots who are at all times wondering what alternative runway they might head to in order to land their plane in an emergency. It is worthwhile to spend time considering how we might survive without any friends, without a reputation, without health, without any love or without much money. Only a few of us will ever write short stories for a living, but very many of us will be called upon by fate to rewrite the stories of our lives. That is the true destiny and function of the imagination.

* * *

It's not easy to picture other lives for ourselves and so – understandably – sometimes we feel like we want to extinguish the one we have. This book seeks to provide alternative scenarios to the ones we have relied on until now – and the strength to move towards them. Suicide is something that a desperate and depleted imagination instinctively likes to turn to, and we shouldn't be terrified if it does drift that way. The Stoics allowed their imaginations to wander a while and their lack of squeamishness at what they found is bracing. We could – of course – end it all. That will always remain the great fallback. But given what we know about the impact of such an act, we should use everything in our power not to do it. Instead, we should be provoked by the intellectual puzzle before us: how can we remain alive, when it would be so easy and so tempting to die? How else might we get by, given how many possibilities have been closed to us? How can we rebuild our futures creatively out of the ruins of our old lives?

iii.

How to Deal with the Meanness
of the World

We live in a world that, much of the time, gives off an appearance of kindness. People say sorry if they bump into us in the street, there's a lot of smiling and gentleness in many homes and offices, modern schools – especially for younger children – devote sincere effort to fostering respect.

This can make it all the more surprising when we discover – in the course of our failure – something that we probably suspected (but tried not to believe) from the outset: that beneath a very thin layer of civility, human beings are capable of extraordinary cruelty. We don't have to wait for a war to break out to realise this; reserves of malevolence and unkindness throb beneath the most innocent circumstances – and are drawn like iron filings to the magnet of failure.

An everyday example of this malevolence can be witnessed in the minor, but telling, arena of comment sections beneath online articles. Here, in anonymity, we encounter the true thoughts of people who might otherwise have smiled or apologised if their umbrella became entangled with ours in the street.

The world's religions have collectively spent billions of hours stressing compassion, forgiveness, generosity, meekness, love, empathy and friendship. Over centuries, they have sought to make progress with our souls. But online comments prove that all efforts at moral education and ethical evolution have made no progress whatsoever. We remain – for the most part – the unkind beasts we always were.

For example, perhaps we read an article explaining that a 30-year-old female prison officer has slept with an inmate a decade younger than she. She is married and has two small children. She has apologised profoundly for a moment of madness, but it didn't help. She was sacked and given a three-year suspended sentence – and barred from employment in most fields. Her husband left her; her father disowned her. She tried to kill herself, failed, but managed to lose an arm in the attempt. A journalist has written up the story and we scroll to the comments:

– *Scum.*
– *Better luck next time.*
– *Unfair! If it had been a man, he would have got a decade behind bars.*
– *What a lenient sentence.*
– *It's sickos like this who run the world.*

This, in a world where people will pick up litter in parks and parents spend time teaching their children to say 'thank you' after someone has passed them a cup of water. Deep down, we harbour impulses that would have made Jesus and the Buddha weep and accept their work had all been in vain.

To protect ourselves against surprise when faced with such facts, we should shed our innocence once and for all. We will be fortified by accepting the grim truth at the earliest opportunity: without any cynical meaning, the truth is that other people – most other people – are simply extremely mean-spirited. Large numbers of humans (what we call 'society at large') are empty of love and tolerance. There may be the odd sentimental effusion here and there, but the rule is that forgiveness and generosity cannot be counted on. Kindness is the firm exception.

Therefore, if and when we fail, we must be ready for nothing less than constant nastiness. It is nothing personal. We should not allow ourselves to assume otherwise, or to be led astray by the present sunny demeanour of people at the dentist's office or the flower shop. Most of our so-called friends will desert us; most strangers will uncritically repeat the worst things said about us; and if a story about us makes it into the papers, most comments written beneath it will need to be read only when we are heavily sedated or in the presence of a doctor or psychotherapist.

If we hear or read vicious statements about ourselves, it is understandable that we might lose our minds or seek to kill ourselves. We would need to be very brutish and coarse inside not to feel such temptations. How could we possibly be brought up to respond well to literature and art, to be open to experience and to be vulnerable in love – and yet somehow not take it as an affront worthy of suicide if we read that we are apparently 'a piece of shit', 'an undeserving pervert', 'someone everyone always hated' or 'a loser who should never have been born'. It takes a degree of insensitivity few of us can or should lay claim to to be able to read such material and assume that life can continue to be some sort of tolerable journey.

In order to try to recover equanimity – as part of our ongoing project to resist a very understandable wish to die – we need to understand what is going on. The meanness has explanations – and the more we have a secure handle on them, the less the meanness will weigh on us. We will still mind, but we will – with luck, when we are well rested – not necessarily be so intensely driven to die.

A crucial step is to recognise that no one would ever be so mean who was not, somewhere inside, extremely unhappy. It wouldn't occur to someone balanced, sane and fulfilled to spit on the defenceless online corpse of their enemy. It wouldn't satisfy anyone who had a sense of purpose, who was loved and who liked themselves, to grind a stranger (however stupid or impulsive they had been) into the dust. Keeping this firmly in our thoughts helps to restore balance in our relationship with our bullying foes. They may seem extremely strong and we may appear defenceless and at their mercy, but their despicable behaviour indicates that they must – inside – be feeling utterly abject and despondent about themselves and their prospects – for only this could explain their glee in our failure. Beneath their confident demeanour, they are wrestling with a sense of overwhelming worthlessness. All schadenfreude is, at heart, a symptom of pain, suffering and a lack of fulfilment. We can't know exactly what the other's problem is, but we can be assured that there is one. And while we may not be able to get back directly at our enemies, by a strange piece of cosmic justice we can know that something or someone has got there first; their behaviour is proof of the scale of their inner misery.

This may seem implausible initially simply because of how widespread the hatred and ill feeling directed at us appears to be. Can we really believe that this level of viciousness could be so common and yet still unjustified? Doesn't it simply indicate that settled public opinion has reasonably decided that we are awful?

Before we panic, however, we should take notice of how widespread unhappiness is – and therefore why it is entirely predictable and logical that 1,000 or even 10,000 horrible comments might be left beneath a story about us in the press, or that a large crowd should be outside the door baying for blood. This degree of meanness isn't a sign of legitimacy; it's evidence of how much misery is in circulation among human beings.

Though the details will vary from case to case, grave disappointment is a constant across populations. The average person, from the moment they wake to the moment they lose consciousness, will be the victim of a stream of slights, large and small – too many almost to register and take issue with, but enough to fill underground cisterns of vengefulness and anger. Their children don't respect them. Their partner no longer admires them. They have been sidelined in their job – which they find repetitive and dispiriting anyway. Their friends are half-hearted in their enthusiasm for them. Their parents let them down. Their house is mediocre, their town in decline. None of it may sound so bad in isolation, but taken together, day after day, there is plenty here to supercharge the batteries of fury and envy.

Much of the time there will be no outlet for this rage. The afflicted person is left to slam the front door, snap at their partner, become impatient with their children or nurse dark thoughts about outsiders. But then, a story of someone else's failure pops up and for a moment there is a satisfying sense that this other person may be to blame for all the disappointments – and their annihilation promises to purify one's own circumstances.

Everyone could, in theory, behave with benevolence and sensitivity. But this doesn't come naturally when a person has had to wait for the bus for forty minutes in the rain, when they haven't had sex in a month, when the boiler has broken again, when three of their good friends earn four times as much as they do, when they have a searing pain in their left knee – and when no one has been properly kind and thoughtful about their life and circumstances for many years.

What may also explain the hatred that descends on us is the extent to which our misdeeds and errors hold a denied, unconscious allure to those who jeer and condemn us most intensely. Our bitterest foes might also, at some level, want to have an affair or leave their family behind. They might secretly desire to get drunk and speak their mind or cheat the accounts. The condemnation is being driven by attempts to pin on one specific person longings that many others share in their depths. They hate in us a disavowed part of themselves.

We might imagine that the way to create a kinder world would be to lecture people on manners and ethics – but what we really need is a world in which everyone is shown sufficient kindness so that stamping on others no longer holds such allure. The true measure of a civilisation is the degree to which people can be good and generous even when no one is watching. This is possible only when they do not feel emotionally exhausted and belittled, because they have been cared for in the past – and so have reserves of tenderness to lend to others in the future.

It is unfortunate that at our moment of failure, it's likely that we will meet with quite so much hatred – that thousands of people may seem keen to deny our remaining claims to humanity just when we need them most. But when the time comes, we must cling to a richer explanation of why this sort of nastiness unfolds. It isn't because we are such awful people (just averagely muddled and sinful ones). Rather, there is no spirit of forgiveness at large because there isn't sufficient love in circulation. We are a mean world because, despite all of our apparent wealth, we are such a limitlessly unhappy one. Our enemies aren't simply cruel, and they definitely aren't correct: they just feel very, very unloved.

iv.

How to Deal with the Meanness
of the Media

If we look at the media from a particular angle, we stand to notice a distinctive fact: almost every story is about failure. What we call a news story is in essence a 'failure story' – someone's marriage has fallen apart, someone's business has gone bankrupt, someone has been fired, someone is involved in a scandal, someone has gone 'mad'.

There is something else. These stories of failure are not, in general, told with any particular imagination or sympathy. Instead, what stands out is the unrelieved viciousness and condemnatory tone on display. If we are to believe the media, all politicians are intrinsically awful, venal, self-interested and actively trying to bring down the nation they claim to care for. People who come to grief in business are monstrous exemplars of greed, exploitation, stupidity and narrow-mindedness. Those who have offended society's moral codes became addicts on purpose, they were hell-bent on having affairs or they actively wanted to hurt their families. Sexual infractions – particular favourites of news organisations – are overwhelmingly the result of 'evil' and 'depravity'. Indeed, most people who feature in the day's news are simply weirdos, perverts and losers. There are never more complex motives. No one is ever profoundly sorry. No one wishes to make amends. No one ever tried hard to be good. No one was ever a child. The appetite is for moral clarity – and the news delivers reliably every time, at the expense of truth and humanity.

In reality, there exist almost no villains of the sort the media presents. An alcoholic is, up close, liable to be filled with repentance and guilt, most politicians would so desperately like to make things better and sexual compulsives are – in their lucid moments – usually appalled by what they have done. The news isn't telling us the facts about people who have failed; it is giving us a window onto our emotional need to locate caricatures.

Long before we ever had news organisations – before there were minute-by-minute bulletins and correspondents in every city – human beings evolved a sophisticated medium for telling stories of failure with a complexity and honesty that modern news organisations never match. In the 4th century BCE, the ancient Greeks gave birth to what we know as 'tragedy' – the art of telling stories of failure with complexity, kindness and moral sophistication. Like news editors, the ancient tragedians picked up on the grimmest stories. They told tales of people who had lied, who had stolen money, who had had affairs, who had slept with members of their families, who had let pride and greed obstruct their judgement. But rather than labelling these figures as weirdos, perverts, reprobates and freaks, the Greeks did something far more interesting: they continued to see them as full and complex human beings, albeit ones who – like all of us – suffered from a fatal flaw in some area or another. The Greeks called this flaw a 'hamartia' – and it was because of a hamartia that a king might poison a rival, or a man might sleep with his mother. Crucially for the Greeks, though, a hamartia did not turn a person into a devil – to view matters like this would be too easy or naïve. The bitter truth that the Greek playwrights wished to convey is that people who end up doing bad things are fundamentally no different from you or me – they are just far less lucky. They get found out for the sorts of things that we have often done ourselves, but which to date we have been able to get away with. They give free rein to impulses that we share but which circumstances have, so far, allowed us to bottle up more securely. The central figures of Greek tragedy aren't worse than anyone else; fate has given their flaws a terrifying window through which to become visible and active in the world.

Our response to hearing of failure and disaster should therefore be compassion for others and fear for ourselves – based on an awareness of how lucky we have been, until now, not to have paid the full price for our own weaknesses of character.

It's a testament to the enduring skill of the great tragedians, in both ancient and more modern times, that the failed characters they have told us about have not become bywords for ignominy and evil – but are instead people whose sorrows deeply concern us and whose cruel fates we bemoan and weep over. It would never occur to us to callously call Oedipus, Antigone, Othello or Tess of the d'Urbervilles freaks or reprobates. We see them in infinitely more rounded ways. We perceive their hamartia, certainly – the strain of greed, lust, impulsiveness, naïvety or selfishness in their character that leads to their downfall – but it is placed alongside other qualities that we are never allowed to overlook. The failed hero we meet in such works of art is also capable of immense kindness, thoughtfulness, wisdom, self-sacrifice and nobility of spirit. Through these stories, we are inducted into a truth that the modern world finds far too uncomfortable to hold on to: that someone might be good *and* flawed, gentle *and* thoughtless, decent *and* compulsive.

If we were to make a list of all the great tragic heroes and their hamartias, we would find that the difference between most of us and them is not the presence of a hamartia, but that we have not yet made the fateful error that gives ours free rein. In this study, we can identify what our own hamartias are and imagine what errors and tragic consequences might develop for us – if ever fate so chose.

Hamartia in Tragedy

Name	Hamartia	Fateful Error	Tragic Consequence
Oedipus	Pride (hubris), anger	Murders his father; sleeps with his mother	Exile, blinded; mother kills herself
Medea	Vengefulness, jealousy	Cannot forgive her husband for starting a new life	Kills her children
Antigone	Stubbornness, loyalty	Disobeys the law; buries her brother	Suicide
Othello	Jealousy	Murders his wife	Suicide
Macbeth	Ambition, greed	Regicide	Wife goes mad and dies; Macbeth murdered
Phèdre	Lust	Sex with her stepson	Shame, guilt; suicide
Arthur Dimmesdale (*The Scarlet Letter*)	Cowardice, lust	Adultery	Disgrace; death
Emma Bovary	Naïvety, romanticism, lust	Adultery; debt; scandal	Outcast; suicide
Anna Karenina	Naïvety, romanticism, lust	Adultery; scandal	Outcast; suicide
What is your hamartia?			

If modern news organisations had reported on the stories of Othello or Oedipus, we can only imagine with what self-righteousness the headline writers would have set to work. 'Love-crazed immigrant kills senator's daughter'; 'Sex with mum was blinding!' We might chuckle darkly at the absurdity of dragging elevated characters like these into the newsroom, as if there was something inherently superior about their stories that would make them unfit for the tabloid writer's pen, but in reality there is nothing about these legendary figures of art that is any different from the wretched characters whom the media inform us about on a daily basis. The only reason why they seem different is that Sophocles and Shakespeare insisted on treating them as rounded humans rather than one-dimensional monsters. Had they, and other great writers (Racine, Tolstoy, Fitzgerald, Eliot, Woolf and so on), had the chance to set to work on the news stories of today, then we would find that there are as many people to weep over, sympathise with and feel pity for today as there were in the canon of Greek or Elizabethan theatre, or the pages of Russian or French literature. Whatever the technical capacities of the authors of tragedies, what is ultimately most impressive is their moral capacity; their ability to look beneath the obvious markers of 'evil' or 'failure' and to detect the human being beneath the murderer, the child within the prisoner, the wise person behind the lunatic. In reality, as these great writers insist to us, there is no such thing as a monster – apart from in the imagination of news organisations and our own over-hasty condemnations. When the media takes care to impress on us that they are telling 'the truth', our consciences should start to signal loudly that something is amiss. We cannot be being told the truth at all. Wherever it is too easy to hate and to mock, the truth has gone missing.

We can put this theory to the test in even the most extreme cases. Let us imagine we come across a story on a news website entitled, 'Weirdo doc guilty of downloading sick porn images'. The news tells us: *A depraved doctor from Sunderland who downloaded more than 1,300 extreme sex images, including scenes of torture and animal cruelty, has been sentenced and jailed for five years. Police found the sickening images on the laptop of Bill Scotch, 34, from Dainsdale Avenue. The doctor, who worked at the town's hospital as a surgeon, earlier admitted to looking at the filthy images. He was sentenced unanimously by the jury and taken away in handcuffs from court.*

Initially, the case seems clear. This man is a devil, and it would be best to lock him in a faraway cell and throw away the keys. But so much of how we respond to people's failure depends on how their story is told. In reality, we would be capable of sympathising with, and feeling sorry for, pretty much anyone – so long as their story was narrated to us in a particular way. As an extreme example, if it were told to us in the way that a visiting angel, Jesus or the Buddha might tell it.

News organisations tend to worry about generating sympathy because they do not trust their audiences to juggle two ideas: that someone could have done a terrible thing for which they will have to spend time in prison – and at the same time, that this person remains a human being. The news can't seem to trust that we might be capable of such two-tiered thinking. Either we have to hate everyone who does anything wrong and then feel happy about their punishment, or else we might see them in more rounded ways and would call for all prison doors to be flung open.

In order to protect us from moral complexity, the news rushes its stories – for the more compressed an account, the less our emotions can be nuanced. It's always the headline that attracts most outrage, while it's no coincidence that the great tragic plays tend to last a few hours and the tragic novels for 400 pages. The more one knows, the harder it is to ridicule and condemn. Even with the bestial doctor, the more we read, the more our emotions might shift:

Condemning the man to his cell, the judge remarked: 'You have thrown away your whole life for the sake of a few hours of gratification. You deserve to be ashamed of yourself forever.' Hearing this, the doctor threw himself on the ground and started wailing – and had to be picked up by the guards. The police informed the court that the man had at first denied downloading the images, then tried to stab himself in the kitchen while officers were upstairs. His wife of three years has taken away their newborn son and asked for a divorce. His own family have disowned him.

Even though we are genuinely horrified by what the doctor has done, it is hard not to shudder when we think of how seven years of medical school, a PhD in a top university and endless hours of work have come to this. An update to the story informs us that the man twice tried to take his life in prison.

None of this is any easier to bear than the plot line of Antigone or Phèdre; we're simply not used to applying a morally complex lens to the figures we are confronted with in the news or to the lives around us. We need to remember the tragic perspective of love, tolerance and forgiveness – both for others and for ourselves, the day we fail.

V.

How to Live with Your Hamartia

When we fail, part of what makes our fate harder to deal with than it needs to be is that we are operating with the idea that a person is essentially either 'good' or 'bad'. We are stuck within a basic binary ethical paradigm – and sadly for us, we may become convinced that, because of what we have done, we are condemned to always be inherently and totally 'bad'.

This is – one might add – the paradigm of children. It never occurs to small children that the adults around them might be a range of opposing things: good and bad, impatient and kind, loving and annoying. The perception of moral complexity belongs to the developing mind. It's a feat of the imagination to be able to see that a good person may do a bad thing, that there may be a difference between what someone does and what they truly meant to do and that an impulse or compulsion is not the same as a reasoned stance.

It is another genius idea of the ancient Greeks that breaks us out of the good–bad paradigm. They insisted on two broad and helpful ideas: all of us mean well and are in that sense fundamentally good – but we are also beset by a multitude of hamartias. In this way, the Greeks arrived at a very subtle ethical stance: we are good, but broken.

This realisation helps us to tolerate ourselves. We certainly may have done and said some truly terrible things, but does this have to make us untenably awful people? No, because there is a difference between our being and our flaws. We are not our flaws. Our flaws shape our lives, but they are not the last word on everything we are. We exist outside of them, however ghastly they may be.

This generous philosophy gives us a little room for mental manoeuvre. We have to atone, we have to take responsibility, we have to despise what we have done and we have to apologise to those we have hurt. But we do not – in the end – have to be without kindness for ourselves.

vi.

How to Deal with the
Pity of Friends

At times of failure, we can expect to be handled with outright disdain and loud hostility by many of the people we encounter. It might, therefore, sound odd to single out as particularly problematic – and especially painful – a kind of treatment that, on the surface, seems like kindness.

When they hear of our disaster, a certain sort of acquaintance will rush to offer us gentle-sounding words. They will ask us with concern how we are doing; they will enquire if they can get us anything at all at what must be a very difficult moment for us; they will say that they can imagine how awful things are and how in agony we must be. They will end a call by entreating us to get in touch with them whenever we want – day or night, weekends too – if they can be of assistance of any kind. They might even briefly sigh and say in a tender voice: 'Poor you!'

How could we be so ungrateful as to mind this treatment, when other people may at this very moment be calling us an idiot, a lunatic or worse? Yet the latter approach might almost be preferable; however bracing, we would at least know where we stood.

What can make honey-coated kindness unbearable is its entanglement with one of the most pernicious emotions we can ever be on the receiving end of: pity. To be pitied is to be placed in a special category of loneliness; to be accorded pariah status at the very moment when what we long for is solace and a confirmation of our right to belong to the human race. The pitying person recognises how desperate our condition is, but what subverts their efforts to be kind is the energy with which they make it clear that our sorrow is ours and ours alone – and that they will not, and could never be, touched by any similar horror. They want to be sweet to us, of course, but what they will not do is recognise that they are as open to foolishness, accident and suffering as we are. Their fear compels them to create a solid wall between our condition and theirs. They need to remind us, and most importantly themselves, that they are firmly rooted on dry land, while we are out there drowning in the ocean swell. Perhaps they will throw us a small life raft – but what they don't want is to imagine ever needing one themselves.

Pity is troubling because it lies so close to something we all desperately want, which is sympathy. Both the pity-bearing and the sympathetic person will say 'poor you'. Both will recognise our troubles, our pain and the extent of our fall. But the pity-bearing person is cruel in their implication that the mess we're in is only ours. They fail to remind us of the crucial truth, which is a great deal more accurate as well as more humane: that we are all, at all times, a hair's breadth away from agony.

The pity-bearing friend reminds us of the distinctiveness of our situation because they are not strong enough to accept the trouble they might face in the future. They may visit us in the hospital, but it's quietly evident that they couldn't ever picture themselves in such a bleak place. They may help us to pay for our groceries, but heaven forbid they would ever one day have to ask a friend for money in turn.

A truly heart-warming and consoling friend is someone robust and mature enough to be reconciled to their own exposure to pain. They know that though they are not on the ward right now, they might easily be soon enough; they understand that everything we are suffering from could touch them one day too – that our sins have echoes in their own hearts. They understand that they haven't been granted immunity from folly and horror; they may be fine right now, but they almost certainly won't be in the end, because life is long and because they are human – and therefore condemned to exquisite kinds of suffering, as we all are. This is the emotional background that will lend their words consolation and their hugs sincerity.

In the end, we should not resent the pity-bearing person. They are not causing us suffering on purpose – and generally they have no clue that they are. They are just very afraid of being like us, not yet accepting that one day they will have to drink from the cup of suffering we've been forced to down. We frighten them; we are ghoulish evocations of everything they are in flight from. When we experience pity, we must remind ourselves that we are not imagining a problem;

we are right to sense how delicately we are being kept at bay, with an imaginary long stick and surgical gloves. Our pity-bearing friend may have called us up to see how we are, but as we take in their well-muffled terror, we should turn the tables on them and reassert our sense of agency and dignity in the face of their sweetly patronising concern. We are explorers of regions that they are still too brittle and apprehensive to travel to – if anyone is in need of a dose of reassuring kindness, it may be them.

vii.

How to Deal with the
Success of Friends

Once we have become failures, we grow acutely conscious of the moments in everyday life in which we can sense afresh the relative good fortune of others – in the small details which, before our downfall, we would scarcely have noticed, let alone been pained by. The most routine chats will be punctuated with unexpected jabs of pain. For example, someone might mention (without any ill will) that they attended an office party, where they gave a little speech thanking their colleagues for their efforts. It might not have been any special kind of triumph – but to us it will be yet another reminder that we have been made redundant, with no hope of finding an equivalent position any time soon. Or someone might remark that they invited the neighbours round for a drink – again, scarcely a boast, but still an agonising signal of social acceptance when we have just been found guilty of fraud and the tale of our felonies is all over the papers. Or perhaps a friend alludes to something funny their teenage child told them, immediately reminding us of the coldly furious manner of our own offspring, bitter about the recent divorce. It doesn't take much to be reminded of the scale of our problems – and the thought of how many ordinary pleasures and routines are no longer available to us. We may even feel jealous of small babies being wheeled around the park by loving parents who pause to ask them if they'd like a drink. Why can't we be them? Why can't our lives be simple and safe? However, instead of feeling jealous of others – friends, babies in the park – we need to feel compassion for the reasons why we aren't them. Our parents were very different; our start set us on a far more arduous path.

The temptation is to make a direct comparison between the lives of others and our own: simply to wish that we could be in exactly their place. To weaken that sentiment, it helps to remind ourselves of the many ways in which we are, and always were, different from those we are presently choosing to compare ourselves to. To look across the aisle and want to swap our lives for theirs is to underestimate the many powerful – and sometimes painful – reasons why we are as we are. The particular travails of our childhood shaped us in very distinctive ways; we had to contend with challenges that others escaped. We haven't merely coped differently with life; we have very different minds. If the people we long to swap lives with had been in our shoes, they might have failed even more gravely than we did.

It may seem as if we are just being envious, but it's more nuanced than that. Envious people are aspirational – they are tortured by the thought of what they *could* have, whether that be greater wealth or fame, houses or love. We are more modest. We know we won't be able to improve our lot; we are on our knees. We just wish we weren't so alone with our peculiar kind of banishment and shame; we wish we weren't the only ones to be thrown into despair by ordinary terms like 'office party', 'holiday', 'cosy evening' or 'family'. We don't want their joy – what we really wish (for our sake, and not because we mean them ill) is that they could have some of our misery.

Unfortunately, we will continue to be constantly tormented until we take measures to protect ourselves. We must face up to our distinctive punishment: to keep ourselves largely apart from other people, because so-called normality is no longer our home and so hurts too much to be part of. The average party will be hell for us; it would be preferable to be sedated and locked up than to attend a school reunion. We're going to need to change our way of socialising to take our failure into account. Excepting those few, rare individuals who are especially skilled at compassion and sympathy, we will need to separate ourselves from everyone who has not – in some significant way – also made a mess of their lives. It sounds radical and one-dimensional, but we will not be doing ourselves any favours by pretending that it is possible to keep up with people who are not comparably wounded. At this time, we are simply not strong enough to deal with the happiness of others. Dating sites and apps have learnt how to match people algorithmically by their interests: golf, comics of the 1950s, the art of Weimar Germany ... It's clear how much shared passions can matter. As failed people, we will have distinctive passions of our own that it will pay to recognise and use as the bedrocks for new forms of socialising. Having reluctantly become world experts in grief and loss, in lying in bed and weeping at our disgraced state, in going over our errors and bemoaning our idiocy, in thinking of killing ourselves and searching for reasons to go on, we should put our skills to work.

There is no point in continuing to spend time with people who are hoping to become partners in their law firm next year and who take their children on skiing holidays. What we need, first and foremost, are people who have banged their heads against the walls from psychological torment and who are getting by with the use of medication or therapy. Though it used to, it doesn't really matter now what else they care or know about. Maybe our new friends never went to university or perhaps they don't read books; they might be pushed to tell us when the Second World War took place (or what it was), or they might have had a career in armed robbery or smuggled cars across the border; maybe they spent a few years on a psychiatric ward. None of that matters in the least. All that counts is that they have suffered a lot and that they have warm and open hearts. We might surprise ourselves by how much closer these new friends become than anyone in our previous life, BF (Before Failure). There is likely to be a lot less grandstanding and one-upmanship. Everyone knows that everyone else is done for; there aren't any prizes for showing off, there are no options to boast or impress.

We will be using friendship to open our hearts, explore our vulnerabilities, speak without inhibition about our insecurities and gain a sense of being helpful through assuaging the pains of others. It's only a pity that we had to lose everything before we at last learnt what other people might be for.

viii.

A Life Devoid of Narcissism

Narcissism – named after Narcissus, the young and handsome Greek mythological figure who was afflicted by an immoderate pride in his own appearance – is a state of mind that is typically condemned and ridiculed by sensible voices. We associate maturity with scepticism towards ourselves, and an inclination towards modesty and self-deprecation.

Nevertheless, a number of psychologists have pointed out the importance of a quality known as 'healthy narcissism' – by which is meant a nourishing, basic level of satisfaction with how we are perceived, how we look and what we have done and said. Healthy narcissism is demonstrated in the little glow we feel when someone pays us a compliment or when we're told that a mutual acquaintance respects us; when we see our name on a report we spent many months working on or when we are invited to contribute to a conference in our professional field. Catching our reflection in a shop window in a city street, we might – as healthy narcissists – feel a little lift at the passing thought that we're looking rather nice at the moment.

Extreme failure shatters every opportunity for this kind of low-level and sustaining self-regard. Narcissism of any sort becomes simply impossible. Given the level of our shame and the amount of condemnation from others, it is hard to think of anything remotely connected with who we are that doesn't make us close our eyes and wince. We cannot bear to think of our past achievements; they merely remind us of our subsequent disasters and idiocies. We are embarrassed to think of everything to do with who we are. Our very name – infamous on the lips of many – frightens us. We avoid the slightest encounters with our own faces. We don't really want to exist as a topic of reflection for ourselves. We come to be about as far away from narcissism, of any kind, as it's possible for a human to be.

So extreme is this stance, that it must be examined for its lessons. Its horrific dimensions are of course evident. It would be so comforting if only we were able to like ourselves a bit more; to hold on to the idea that we are not only a monster or a fool; to have access to some echo of the feeling we had in childhood when we were told we were good and sweet, when we were cuddled and our hair was stroked. But our self-censoring mechanisms no longer allow it. We cannot have an agreeable past, future or present. Our essential self is contaminated and therefore something we are impelled to ignore.

Through this emotional turmoil, however, we unexpectedly come close to a state of mind lauded by the most accomplished sages of the Buddhist tradition. For Buddhists, ultimate enlightenment is reached when we finally manage to obliterate the self and see the world without the distracting, petty and vain distorting lens of the 'I'. For a true sage, who we happen to be is an entirely random and negligible accident, which we must strive to move beyond; it shouldn't matter what we look like, how others perceive us, whether we were born rich or poor, what people are saying about us or how long we will live. All that counts is to pierce the veil of immediate and petty illusion in order to attune ourselves to the broadest totality of being: to take our place as an observer of cosmic reality. A sage will strive (through exhaustive meditative practices) to forget everything about their self; they seek to merge with the universe and take their rightful, anonymous, temporary place alongside wind, rocks, the raging oceans and billions of dying stars.

Through the most ghastly process, we will have entirely overcome ourselves. Without subscribing to any spiritual groups, we'll have managed to focus single-mindedly on things beyond us. This isn't what anyone but a few die-hard monks might be seeking, but there is – arguably – a degree of genuine achievement behind our exquisite pain. We now endure in a curious, liminal space: we can't really exist to ourselves any more, and yet we are still obliged to be alive. Unlike most other people on the planet, we are extensively dissociated from our own being; we can't think of our bodies, our pasts, our futures or our selves in the minds of others. None of that matters – or it is, more accurately, past bothering with. We are instead entirely focused on what is beyond us; pure observers of the world outside of ourselves.

For Buddhists, this kind of liberation is an end in itself. For us, it threatens – on its own – to be a hollow and eerie state. We need to convert it into the first step towards a more redemptive and tolerable condition: a life that we can live in the service of causes that are somehow 'larger' than we are. We'll have fulfilled the promise of our pain and self-abnegation when we succeed in placing something compellingly meaningful at the centre of our scarred lives: a deserving cause beyond us. It might be a job, a project, a suffering child or adult … We have no option but to forget ourselves and to live for others.

ix.

Living with Permanent Infamy

When search engines first came into prominence in the late 1990s, they promised to correct one of our minds' greatest flaws: amnesia. It would no longer matter if we forgot the way back home, the name of the local hardware store or the date of Napoleon's Russian campaign. The internet would have the missing information ready for us in milliseconds.

What most people overlooked, however, was that this relentless ability to remember everything – and forget nothing, even the B-side of a particular Beatles single, the name of Marcus Aurelius's mother or the road from Ipswich to Lowestoft – would eventually have the power to trail and torment us into eternity if we were ever unlucky or foolish enough to err.

The internet has become an eternal charge sheet and bulletin board of every human being's record of disgrace, failure and idiocy. Twenty years after an infraction, the internet still reminds everyone about what we did and how others judged it – and the misdemeanour is as shocking and disappointing as it ever was. It doesn't matter if, in the intervening period, we have transformed our character, apologised to everyone involved, adopted a new religion or purged our soul. In the implacable opinion of the internet, we are fated to forever be our own worst moment – as captured by a journalist, or even just a passing stranger armed with a mobile phone and social media account, untrained in the empathetic methods of a Greek playwright. The curious barman at the hotel, the bank employee, the family at the next table – all are able to tap into their phone and know. We can never be a 'nobody' or even a 'somebody quite nice'; we are always and forever the disgrace we once were.

As a society, we have over the years grown sensitive to the burden placed on individuals by prejudices and biases around race, gender and background. We have become aware of how crushing it is to disappear into a ready-made negative category in someone's mind, and associate civilisation with a community in which everyone has the opportunity to escape summary and be discovered anew. It may sound obscene to compare the innocent victims of prejudice with the often-deserved opprobrium directed at those who have failed – yet we might at least propose that a civilised society should know when to curtail punishment. Just as we accept that there should be a prison 'term' – that after two or five or twenty-five years someone should have served their time – so we might propose that there should be a defined end to the punishment of infamy.

Yet if internet-enabled infamy remains lifelong, it's partly because most of us fail to see it in the same way we would a prison sentence: we can intuitively understand why having to subsist in a bare, ugly cell should count as a severe chastisement, but we may never have taken the time to reflect on the distinctive burden constituted by infamy. We might even complain that someone who is merely mocked and shunned but has not gone to prison has got off lightly. Yet a moment of reflection should show us that infamy is very much its own burden and not a negligible one at that. As infamous people, we may, theoretically, be able to travel anywhere we like, but we will always be judged in the same entirely damning way. We will always be imprisoned within the negative assumption of others; we will never be able to spring open the door of the cage of suspicion and condemnation. And what's worse, there will never be a judge who can say that now enough is enough; never a jury that will reconsider the facts and set us free. Infamous people are put in cells and the keys thrown away.

The punishment of the infamous is endless because it exists in a public mind that is continuously informed by the eternal memory of the internet – and that never sees any reason to doubt what it reads. After all, if this magical internet is able to summon the exact map coordinates we require or the precise cost of a new lamp, why would we ever doubt its ability to give us the correct information about the weirdo at the next table or the ridiculous candidate we were considering interviewing for a job. No counter-narrative can ever be built that will be powerful enough to control the floodwaters of damning online data. Shakespeare or Sophocles could write the finest drama about our fate, but for the average person with a phone we would still be the disgusting person who deserved every hateful comment accorded by a journalist twenty-two years ago.

It is worth registering this problem – but certainly not worth hoping for anything to change any time soon. Evolution here is measured in centuries. It took the better part of 1,000 years for humanity to realise that it was probably not a good idea to put people in stocks. In the medieval Netherlands, arriving late to church would result in one being draped in 'stones of shame' – large rocks linked by a heavy metal chain. In medieval Austria, spouses accused of being 'argumentative' were locked in a 'shrew's fiddle', a portable pillory that locked the hands upwards in front of the face; an attached bell let the townspeople know that a 'shrew' was approaching so that they could run out of their homes and mock her. The good old days!

In the 14th–16th centuries, women across Europe could be disgraced for cuckolding or scolding their husbands, or for bearing an 'illegitimate' child. Punishment was often by the 'cucking stool' or 'ducking stool', a large wooden armchair fixed to a wooden arm over a lake or river; the accused would be ducked as many times as her alleged crime dictated. Often, she did not survive.

The most common form of public humiliation around this time was when a convicted criminal was restrained in a pillory (a wooden frame with holes for the head and hands) and displayed in a public place, where they could not hide from the jeers, abuse and rubbish that were thrown at them. The crowd were expected to demonstrate their disgust with the convict – if the crime was particularly heinous or offensive, they might have rotten eggs and slaughterhouse waste

Top: A shrew's fiddle, or neck violin, 18th century
Bottom: Illustration of a ducking stool from an 18th-century chapbook

flung at them. For this reason, pillories were usually placed at the busiest site in a town or city – at the intersection of two major streets or roads, in the marketplace or town square, or in front of a church. In London in 1810, six men were pilloried for two days for 'sodomy'; the City had to pay 252 constables to stand guard and protect them from an enraged mob, who nevertheless pelted the men with mud, dead cats, rotten eggs and vegetables, blood, offal and dung. The pillory remained a standard judicial sentence for sedition, homosexuality, extortion, fraud and perjury in Britain until 1837.

Numberless variations of these kinds of instruments of punishment were devised. The 'scold's bridle' was designed to inhibit speech and feeding by means of a piece of metal that depressed the tongue, and it was commonly used in England and Scotland in the 16th and 17th centuries as a 'minor' punishment for women found guilty of scolding or gossiping.

The jougs was an iron neck-collar and chain attached to a church wall, commonly used in Scotland. Those found guilty of offences like drunkenness, gossiping or missing church would be placed in the jougs and made to beg forgiveness from their neighbours passing in and out of the church.

In other words (lest we doubted it), we are a limitlessly judgemental species that appears to gain a lot of relief from our disappointments by hating others, without measure, for being 'bad'. We should not add to our sorrows by imagining that we might be living in a forgiving world.

Top: A scold's bridle, 17th–18th century
Bottom: Jougs, Sorn Church, East Ayrshire, Scotland, c. 17th century

The good news is that we are also highly adaptable. We love having two legs, but, if fate were to decree it, we'd end up being able to get by on one. It's very nice not to have to sit in urine-stained underpants, but you can tell someone they need their bladder removed and they'll generally keep living and be grateful for the chance to do so. It's nice to speak, of course, but people can and will endure having their voice box removed and having to talk through an electronic replacement. Possibilities that seem hugely difficult to cope with from a distance have a habit – once we have to go through them – of proving survivable. It's not what we would have chosen, for sure, but we cope. We may be the person who everyone in the community hates and mocks and thinks evil, but we can take it. Every time we walk into a room, we can be sure that ninety-eight per cent of the people there are sniggering – and yet we hold on to reasons to keep living.

That's the level of pain we need to be ready for.

There are upsides to amnesia. If we can allow ourselves to forget, we can also cease to torture ourselves with comparisons between what we once had and what we have now. We won't remember or dwell too much on what it was like to have two legs or a functioning bladder or a name that wasn't dirt. We can inhabit the present; the past is another country whose outlines can be left to grow blessedly vague.

When we are infamous, very few people will want to talk to us. Our interactions with 'most people' will be sharply curtailed. It is at this point that we will discover that the only people whose time and interest we can really hold out for are those who know about something that is widely esteemed but almost never understood: love.

x.

What Love Really Is and
Why It Matters

There is so much talk of love in our societies; it would be natural to think that by now we must know what it is and why it counts. Love, we think, is the excited feeling we get in the presence of someone of unusual accomplishment and talent – great intelligence or beauty for the most part – who we hope will reciprocate our interest and whom we badly want to touch, caress and one day share our lives with. This definition sounds so plausible and enjoys such powerful cultural endorsement that we are apt to miss another vision of love altogether – this one focused not so much on an appreciation of strength as on a tolerance of, and kindness towards, what is weak and misshapen.

According to this alternative vision, we display love when, for example, on the way home, we come across an itinerant drunk –

weather-beaten and dishevelled, beer-addled and ranting – and do not turn away, but instead take the momentous internal step (with all the eventual outward actions that might follow) of considering them as a version of ourselves, prey to the same passions and distempers, visited by the same longings, upset by similar losses and worthy of their own share of compassion and tolerance.

We show love, too, when we see a well-dressed person shouting imperiously at an airport, filled with self-righteousness, apparently bloated on their own self-regard, and do not dismiss them immediately as insane or entitled, but instead, take the trouble to see the frightened, vulnerable self beneath the bluster. When we grow curious as to the sickness of the soul that might be operating just below the surface and are able to wonder what has hurt them – and why they might be so scared.

It is love that sparks within us when we see a small child throwing themselves on the floor in the aisle of a supermarket, shouting that they want 'it' again and again, and do not simply focus on how inconvenient it is to steer our trolley around them and how piercing and maddening their screams are, but also feel how much we understand their frustration – and long to tell them that their pain is, in its general form, our own.

It is also love – the proper and most serious variety in the universe – when our partner is being plainly irrational, unfair, mean-spirited and maddening, and yet we do not, as we so easily might, launch a full dose of righteous anger their way, but instead hold back a little and wonder why this formerly sane and interesting adult should have fallen apart in this manner. When we contemplate the idea that they are not merely awful and vicious, but instead might not have slept very well last night, are perhaps panicked by what the future might bring them or might inside be dealing with feelings of lacerating self-contempt that they hardly understand, let alone know how to master. It is love to go up to them and extend our arms at precisely the juncture when we have so many reasons to slam the door in their face.

However many songs celebrate the act, it is no particular feat to love someone who is on their best behaviour, who looks beautiful and who moves with grace through the world. What really cry out for our attention and our love are rather those people and things that are crooked and gnarled, damaged and self-disgusted. In this definition, love is the effort required to accurately imagine oneself in the life of another human – one who has not made it in any way easy to admire or even like them.

It is love when a novelist spends 300 pages detailing the interior life of a violent criminal and allows us to see the innocent child within the guilty adult. In the Christian tradition, it was the man from Nazareth who gave us the most memorable demonstrations of this sort of love – who made it seem glamorous to love differently from the Romans and the Greeks; to love the prostitute, the prisoner and the sinner, to show love to a wretch and an enemy. To extrapolate from this approach, we might imagine that a truly Christian dating app would not merely highlight the beautiful and the dazzling or allow us to swipe away every slightly displeasing person at a stroke, but would instead stop us arbitrarily at photographs of more challenging figures – those shunned by society, shocking reprobates – and command, with all the authority of divine intonation, 'Love! Here where it would feel so natural and so easy to hate, your duty is to love ...'

That such a command sounds peculiar and laughable is a measure of how we have forgotten this sort of love and how committed we are to love-as-admiration. Yet it is possible to suggest that nothing is more important than this love – that this is the love that rescues nations from intolerance, that pauses wars, that halts recriminations, that calms furies, that prevents murders and that allows civilisation to continue. True love involves precisely *not* giving someone what is their due but giving them what they need in order to survive instead.

Not least, the spirit of love demands that we acknowledge how much we ourselves may one day stand in need of this form of love-as-forgiveness. We cannot rely on always having justice on our side, in always being able to make a claim on others based on our own unsullied righteousness and goodness. At some point, we may well have to cry for mercy. We may have no leg to stand on. We may have behaved foolishly, and might be in line for severe punishment from a judge who closely follows the letter of the law. At this point, we should hope that there is someone around who still remembers what true love is. Someone who will undertake the heroic effort of not giving us what we deserve, but rather recalling that there must be a sweet and distinctly blameless child beneath the horrible and difficult adult we have become. Someone who can bypass the jeering mob and offer us counsel and reassurance, knowing that every human has a claim upon forgiveness and imagination.

Perhaps, by this example, we will in turn become people who know how to love properly – and after our particular crisis has passed, we may make the effort to extend love to others who have transgressed, so that society can – through this enriching mutuality of imagination – become a less frightening and less harried place for all. A place in which we know to treat one another like naughty children who can be redeemed, rather than felonious wrongdoers who must be loathed into eternity.

xi.

Let Him Who Is without
Sin Cast the First Stone

We are so used to thinking of Jesus as a divinity whom we accept or reject on the basis of faith, that we are apt to miss a far more relevant detail: he was an extremely acute philosopher, whose directions on human conduct maintain a deep applicability.

One of the most salient of Jesus's secular lessons comes in chapter eight of the Gospel According to John. Jesus has recently come down from Galilee to Jerusalem when some Pharisees – members of a sect focused on precise adherence to Jewish tradition and law – present him with a married woman whom they have caught having sex with someone other than her husband. 'Teacher,' they ask him, 'this woman was caught in the very act of committing adultery. In our law, Moses commanded that such a woman must be stoned to death. Now what do you say?'

Jesus is being edged into a trap. Will he say that it is completely fine to have an affair (in other words, to condone something that his society regards as very wrong)? Or will the mild-mannered preacher of love and forgiveness turn out to be just as strict about legal matters as the Jewish authorities he likes to criticise?

Jesus makes a deft move. He doesn't categorically deny the mob the right to stone the woman to death – but he adds one apparently small, but in practice epochal, caveat to this right. They can stone her to their hearts, content if, and only if, they can be absolutely sure that they have first satisfied one crucial criterion: they have never done anything wrong themselves.

By this, Jesus doesn't mean just that they have never slept around outside of their marriage – he means if they have never done anything wrong *at all*, whatsoever, in any area of their lives. Only absolute moral purity, Jesus suggests, grants us the right to be vicious, high-handed and unsparing towards transgressors. An important principle of ethics is being introduced here: we can only be counted as properly innocent when we have done nothing wrong whatsoever, at any point and in any context – not simply when we are blameless in one area or another. If we have slipped up in any field, even one very far removed from the crime at hand, then we are duty bound to stretch our powers of empathy, to strive to identify with the wrongdoer and to show them an advanced degree of mercy and charity. We may not have committed the particular crime they are being punished for, but we are implicated in sin more generally – and therefore must forgive.

Jesus responds to the Pharisees with what have become immortal words: 'Let him who is without sin cast the first stone.' The mob, understanding the rebuke, put down their projectiles and the terrified woman is spared.

The real target of this story is a perennial problem in the human soul, self-righteousness, which is itself the degenerate outgrowth of something otherwise extremely valuable: a desire to be in the right. The problem is that being in the right in some areas has a fateful tendency to lead us to see ourselves as morally blameless across our entire lives – and therefore encourages a particular mean-spiritedness and inhumanity towards those who transgress in situations where we have been good. Our impeccable position on, say, the economy, or poverty or the right way to run a household can give us grounds for viewing ourselves as morally blameless in and of ourselves – a stance from where extraordinary cruelty can follow.

Jesus's point is that the surest way to be kind is not to take pride in never having committed a particular kind of wrong, but rather to see that, inevitably, we too have been foolish and cruel at other moments – and to use that knowledge to foster compassion towards those whom it lies in our powers to 'stone'. A world in which we keep our own wrongs firmly in mind becomes, paradoxically, a truly virtuous and humane place.

xii.

Bourgeois Respectability

Since the middle of the 17th century, starting in the Netherlands and then expanding around the continent, the educated middle classes of Europe have aspired to an ideal of sobriety and decency that has been captured by the term 'bourgeois respectability'. Lawyers, doctors, traders and professionals of every kind have tried to distinguish themselves from the perceived decadence of aristocrats on the one hand and the permissiveness and chaos of the working classes on the other. To be a respectable bourgeois has meant having a tidy house, going to bed early, reading serious books, taking long bracing walks in cold air, teaching one's children manners, dressing well but unostentatiously and harbouring a fierce hatred of public disorder. But more than such outward details, it has also meant keeping a close eye on one's passions, never giving way to impulse or appetite, following the rules and obeying the moral code set by one's society. It means taking an extraordinary interest in maintaining an unsullied reputation and in trusting in the rectitude of public life, especially in the opinions set out by significant figures in the newspapers. At the funeral of a respectable bourgeois, one of the chief points of praise might be that the deceased led an exemplary, upright existence – and was supremely well thought of by the entire community.

It is easy to mock, but that would be to miss out on the charms of bourgeois life and the substantial achievements it has produced. It is profoundly gratifying to have a neat laundry cupboard, carefully ironed clothes and a well-arranged kitchen; to have a good name among a wide range of polite and hard-working friends and to gather at dinner time around well-prepared and nutritious meals; to have enough but not too much money – and to spend it in carefully judged amounts on objects and projects of lasting value.

In Clemens Bewer's portrait of the lawyer and civic official Johann Janssen and his family, painted in Aachen during Germany's 19th-century middle-class ascendancy, we find a celebration of the bourgeois ethos. Johann stares out in a quiet but resolute way at the viewer; this is a man sure to have sensible opinions on all legal and financial matters: he might make an excellent godfather and would know how to recommend the purchase of the right kind of solid and well-crafted dining chairs. At the end of a particularly long, hot summer day, he might take off his cravat and relax in the garden with a very small glass of locally sourced Riesling. His wife, Magdalena, looks after the children. She appears timid, sensible and entirely fulfilled by domestic tasks. The children would likely know to say please and thank you. The little one (holding her mother's hand)

Clemens Bewer, *Johann Wilhelm Janssen and His Family*, 1843

might be the butt of family jokes because of her habit of sometimes speaking out of turn – but by the time she turns six, these kinks will have been ironed out, and she will look forward to following her mother in heartfelt domestic devotion and good behaviour.

Unfortunately for us, bourgeois respectability is – naturally – entirely incompatible with failure. One cannot be both a respectable bourgeois and involved in a scandal, both a bourgeois and a divorcee, both a bourgeois and mentally unwell or both a bourgeois and bankrupt. Nor in the bourgeois worldview is there much room for redemption; one wouldn't work quite so hard at keeping up appearances if it were really possible to pick oneself up from a fall and begin afresh. There are codes of responsibility and accountability that cannot be bypassed. Johann Janssen would have studiously avoided us if we had failed.

What, then, can happen to the shamed bourgeois, exiled from the garden of respectable existence?

Traditionally, there has been one refuge – what has been termed 'bohemia'. Bohemia is the opposite of, but also the logical correlate to, the bourgeois realm. In the eyes of the bourgeois, bohemia embodies everything there is to be scared about. The worst that could happen to one's child, worse than death perhaps, is that they should end up living as a bohemian, in an attic somewhere at the top of a building on the bad side of town, aspiring to write novels or plays or paint pictures, engaged to an actor, wearing unironed clothes and eating food without cutlery or even a plate. Paintings of bohemian

Octave Tassaert, *Studio Interior*, 1845

life produced around the same time as Janssen's family portrait were meant to strike terror into bourgeois hearts – and they did.

Contemplating these two opposing poles, we might find ourselves not overly enamoured of either. We might be put off by the narrowness and moralism of bourgeois life, but also frightened by the mess and discomforts of bohemia.

In the wake of failure, however, we would do well to hang on to the better sides of both philosophies – while leaving out the problematic ones. There is much to learn from either side; from bohemia, we gain a necessary scepticism towards public opinion, we learn not to give too much of a damn what the neighbours think and are invited to take our own ideas and inclinations more seriously – and we also learn not to equate a bad reputation with inherent shamefulness. The bohemians allow us to believe that we might fall short of society's ideals of decency and yet, at the same time, continue to have the right to live. Our name might be an object of suspicion among lawyers and doctors, but we might still have one or two things to contribute.

At the same time, from the bourgeois, we can pick up a due appreciation of order and domesticity. We can learn to take pride in a well-kept home in spite of having chaotic inner feelings and a complicated private life. Indeed, it's precisely because of these areas of confusion that we especially esteem a tidy cupboard and a well-laid table.

After failure, we might not be accepted back into the bourgeois circle – but we are at least provided with a moment to reflect upon both the achievements and the limitations of this dominant, now-triumphant approach to life. Going forward, we can instead aspire to hold on to a carefully edited mixture of bourgeois and bohemian virtues.

xiii.

Practical Measures

Though much of the adjustment we must make to deal with failure is psychological – a question of adjusting how we see ourselves, how we interpret the past and how we frame our defeat – a good share of the challenge is also practical – concerning decisions around money, friendship, occupation and housing. In a bid to fail well, we should consider some of the following themes.

Our name

Starting from when we are very little, our name tends to be powerfully associated in our own minds with the seat of our true identity. Though it was only chosen by our parents – perhaps after a slightly haphazard process of deliberation – to us, as children, it can seem as if a divine force or some sagacious higher authority picked it out; as though there must be a necessary and indelible connection between who we are and what we are called. As we learn to write our name at nursery school, carefully shaping the letters in a selection of different coloured pens, we build up a connection between our name and our essential self, as symbolised by such elements as our toes, our sense of humour, the way we blink in the sun and our memories of our first seaside holiday. This will be the name that our first lovers will use, that our friends will tweak when they tease us affectionately, that we will write down on application forms for jobs and mortgages ... The idea of changing this name, intentionally, in the wake of a disaster, can therefore sound as odd as attempting to alter the animal species we belong to.

What's more, the sort of people who usually change their names do so in circumstances we would hesitate to identify with: major criminals, ex-Nazis, runaway felons ... Their motives for changing their names seem to be connected with outright deception and crookedness. Are we really to join the ranks of the sinister name-changers?

But before we reject the proposal definitively, we might take a moment to think about the psychology of lying. There are situations in which the act of lying should not be counted as an automatic offence. We are sometimes justified in offering a so-called white lie when the truth is at risk of being unhelpfully and gravely distorted by prevailing rigid or categorical ideas. We may lie to preserve the vital truth, through a minor act of fabrication or omission. For example, if a favourite aunt asks us if we like the cake she has baked for us, we might tell her that it's delicious, not because it is, but because the unvarnished facts about the cake would set off such an avalanche of doubts in our relative's mind that it would take the relationship further from the truth than a small deception about icing and moisture. Alternatively, we might decide to hide our religion from a new acquaintance for a while because we know that the revelation of our faith would at once close down a dialogue that is of value to us both; one day we will get around to mentioning the truth, but we need to wait for the reality of our character and the sincerity of our intentions to get across before endangering these via a small, yet sadly unavoidably explosive, fact. Sometimes, the preservation of a larger truth requires us to walk through the gate of a minor lie.

By analogy, our failure can mean that our name immediately triggers a response in other people that is genuinely unwarranted and substantially untrue to who we actually are. The name might make them think that we are about to steal their partner (because we were once involved in an adulterous scandal), or that we may try to make off with their wallet or their car keys (because we were once caught up in a tax fraud at a company we worked at twenty years before). The mention of our name will mean that our reality is at once lost and replaced by a one-dimensional caricature. We won't have a chance to share anything of what we are actually like; our new acquaintance will have fled before getting to know us was even an option.

In such circumstances, we might well wonder whether it would be a good idea to change our name, so as to give us more of an opportunity for a fair hearing. Of course, in time – if an interaction deepens – we can fill people in on our life story, but only once they are in a better position to see us in a rounded way.

In many a fairy tale, a royal – burdened by the weight of expectation attached to their name – will pretend to be a commoner, not in order to manipulate, but in order to achieve a more sincere connection with others that would be impossible if their impactful title were known from the start. The royal lies in order to be more truthfully known. Our own name change will in effect be like a grimmer version of the same phenomenon. We, too, will hide who we are, not to mock or taunt, but to attempt to be sincere and true. With no egregious or criminal intentions in mind, we might well become 'someone else', so as to keep alive more of who and what we actually are.

Exile

It's a rather odd motive for travel; we don't much hear of it as a reason why someone would decamp to another corner of the world. We're familiar with a search for better weather, for richer work opportunities, for greater proximity to family ... But what isn't mentioned is that we might be impelled to move because we are simply too exhausted and internally weighed down – by people's stares, by the words that we know will be exchanged every time we leave a room or a shop, by the 10,000-ton 'story' we are invisibly dragging around behind us at every step.

What can be appealing about another country is the sheer indifference of the population. They – blessedly – are too preoccupied with their own dramas to give a damn about us. Their newspapers – written in a language we don't understand – are filled with quite different stories; here there are other actors, politicians, business people and lovers getting in trouble in different ways. Here we can lose ourselves in the crowd. First and foremost, we are just another foreigner. The details of our story don't matter. Aside from a few exceptions, the people don't expect to get to know us; we are merely 'the outsider' – we stand outside of their status system and hierarchies of respect and honour.

So, finally, we can be left in peace. We can sit in a cafe with the local beverage or soup and watch an unfamiliar world go by. There will be different sorts of barbers, the people will shop in quite different ways and the streets will be filled with other aromas.

In the olden days, all that would have been needed was to go over to another valley or to the next city along. Nowadays, we may have to move a whole continent or two. We are often asked to celebrate how small the world has become; what a little village it is, thanks to our planes and technologies – but what a burden villages can be the moment there is gossip, scandal or failure. It is a true luxury that there still exist different areas in the world that care not as much for one another as they eventually will. The human mind can't hold all the defeats of every member of the species in mind at one moment; failure remains relatively local if we are fortunate. Once upon a time, we'd have taken a ship to San Francisco or Sydney. With what gratitude we'd have sailed past Bradley's Head to set up home in Kurraba Point, where we could admire the eucalyptus trees and the sound of spotted pardalotes; how lucky we would have been that it took six months for the London newspaper to arrive, and even then, they might leave out the more gossipy bits – or not connect the dots. How claustrophobic the internet and the plane have rendered our lives. One day, there may be different planets to head to, and we can be first in line for a trip to Pluto or for the colonisation of Neptune. We are in a strange and sad interregnum: the planet increasingly too small for failure, the universe still closed for escape. But even now, there are teeming capital cities at far ends of the globe that can provide refuge – places that we will be able to call home not because we speak the language or understand the ways, but precisely because we will be total aliens and because in such obscurity who we really are has a chance to emerge, shielded from the constant stares and violent hatreds of our native villages.

Social life

In the normal course of things, we want friends who are interesting, beautiful, fun and – ideally – prestigious. After failure, the requirements get a lot stricter. What we need first and foremost are people who will not judge, who will not moralise and who will know how to forgive.

There is no single route down which the human mind must go in order to reach this psychological sweet spot, but it's possible to suggest a likely trajectory. Fundamentally, to accept failure, a person has to have experienced grave suffering at the hands of the dominant societal hierarchy. Something needs to have loosened them from, or rendered them suspicious of, the prevailing status system.

Maybe, at a young age, their particular sort of intelligence was not recognised by the school system. They therefore know intuitively what it is like to be labelled a failure – and how unfairly the tag can be applied. Or perhaps they were at odds with a parent who bullied them or made them feel small for not performing well according to measures that were ultimately arbitrary and disconnected from who they were. Perhaps their sexuality set them at odds with the popular ideals of their communities; they knew that their tastes meant that they could never be simply 'ordinary' and lightly accepted. Or, more likely and ideally still, they are people who have themselves slipped up and been exposed. They have known what it is like to wake up one day and have a damning crowd outside the door, to have the internet in flames against them, to be shown the office door after a terse meeting with the boss or to be cast aside by family and abandoned by their social circle. The friends one makes after failure will be those who are fully inducted into the meanness of the human heart. They will have suffered unbearably, been ostracised and judged. They will have spent time sobbing in lonely bedrooms.

Most of us mean to be kind, but we are never punished long or hard enough actually to become so. In the end, ex-prisoners are probably some of the greatest sorts of new friend we can make. There is no more broad-minded set of people on Earth. Their experience wears down all self-satisfaction and arrogance; they are devoid of pride and at the same time, utterly able to recognise our own hunger for sympathy. Maybe at one point they robbed banks or drove getaway cars, but they have the qualities (so long as they are no longer actively involved in crime) to be the gentlest and most imaginative friends. It takes someone who has lost contact with their family and been disowned by their social circle to really understand love. There is no point seeking out 'good people' among the blameless and the innocent. We need to nourish our hunger for friendship from richer, more potent sources.

Once we are ready for friendship after a failure, we would do well to seek out ex-burglars and ex-con artists, ex-hijackers and ex-tax evaders. There should be groups specifically focused on connecting those who have failed with this vibrant, redemptive sort of community. Their souls – if we are lucky – will be ready to receive and honour our own distinctive needs for charity.

Love life

Failure is a cleansing agent for relationships. It is ruthless with all but the most solid bonds; it gets rid of all but the most sincere. Failure works out what love is worth keeping – and ensures that other varieties are extinguished in short order. It won't tolerate simulacrums of love – the flattery that can pass for it, or the sentimental attachment or unfocused crush.

There are plenty of apparently viable unions that can, in benevolent times, go on forever – out of habit, a longing for security or a fear of what the neighbours would think. But once there is shocking failure – once the neighbours are mocking anyway, once our craving for tenderness reaches a pitch, once we lose any hesitation about asking for hugs and caresses, once we are crying like small children and don't mind saying what is actually on our minds – we quickly see which love is worth preserving and which never merited the name in the first place.

The partner who might have stayed with us out of convenience or because – for a long time – we were a handy route to money and status, will hardly make a protest (or only a tiny one, in order to preserve their own dignity). They will let us go soon enough; they never signed up to a mess, they never thought they would be asked to care without much hope of reward (except for thoughtful gratitude). They understood love as being with someone who could shore them up and make them feel better. It wasn't about nailing themselves to a loser.

It would be better to keep such criteria in mind from the beginning of any future dating process. We should ask ourselves: is this a person who would stay by me when everyone else is laughing, who wouldn't run away if I had no more money, who would stick around if I had enemies or was driven off to jail ...? These are not normal questions to wonder about on a first date – we're meant to look into their eyes and wonder about their job prospects – but they are the qualities we should turn over in our minds given the role of fate and the presence of our hamartia. We are not looking for dumb or uncritical loyalty; what we aspire to is a sort of love that recognises us in our totality and respects the workings of fortune – and is therefore slower to judge or to flee.

In honour of these concerns, we might, on a future date, ask our partner: 'And how might you feel about waiting for me until I end a prison term?' Most would immediately look horrified and run away. A few will smile and utter a gentle 'but of course' – and we'll know then never to let them go.

The solace that these types of people can bring us is beyond compare. When failure strikes, they will compensate for the love of the whole world. One person's close and attentive ministration can truly make up for the unsteady adulation and eventual cruel condemnation of millions. It won't matter very much at all that we are ridiculed by strangers, if we are taken seriously by the one person we esteem in our own home. We'll know exactly what Shakespeare meant in his 'Sonnet 29', even if not every word makes it through from his Elizabethan English to our own:

When, in disgrace with fortune and men's eyes,
I all alone beweep my outcast state,
And trouble deaf heaven with my bootless cries,
And look upon myself and curse my fate,
Wishing me like to one more rich in hope,
Featured like him, like him with friends possessed,
Desiring this man's art and that man's scope,
With what I most enjoy contented least;
Yet in these thoughts myself almost despising,
Haply I think on thee, and then my state,
(Like to the lark at break of day arising
From sullen earth) sings hymns at heaven's gate;
For thy sweet love remembered such wealth brings
That then I scorn to change my state with kings.

With this very particular sort of lover in our lives, the sort that would wait outside the prison gates for us, we'll finally be in a position to understand love. We'll know that kings – or more realistically, celebrities and tech millionaires – don't have anything on us and that, despite the mess we have made of our lives, we are the luckiest people on the Earth.

Jobs

After a downfall, what are we to do with ourselves workwise? If we can get another job, what sort of job should it be?

Usually, in even the noblest minds and most virtuous professions, work is seldom without a degree of vanity. A doctor wants to help their patients, for sure, but they are also quietly pleased when they are noticed doing so by prestigious eyes. A charity worker is concerned with the war-torn country they are helping, but they are forthright when asking for a raise as well. Most jobs allow workers to engineer moments when they can be admired and acclaimed slightly more than would be warranted by the strict needs of the job itself.

This, of course, is impossible – and sickening – for those who have failed. When we have suffered a downfall, we see work not as a place to stand out, but instead to disappear. Hopes of personal glory are firmly behind us. What we want to be subsumed by is something very distinctive and very wise: *problems far larger than our own*. As failed people, we are likely to be in the market for the enormous problems of other people; we want to work long and hard at something very serious that leaves no room either for showing off or for thinking of ourselves. We need to find difficulties so urgent, so ghastly, so serious, so indisputably critical that we will – while attending to them – be able to forget who we are and what has happened to us. It really won't matter that we were sacked or disgraced or humiliated when a house is on fire, when one of the patients in a hospice needs a defibrillator, when we have to get an ambulance up a hillside to rescue a stricken child, when we're trying to alleviate malaria in an under-nourished population in a war-ravaged country or when we are assisting on a ward filled with people who are seeking to take their own lives.

Such work will leave us feeling exhausted, rocked to the core and sometimes traumatised – but what it will not do is remind us of what we have lost and how much fashionable society once respected us. Indeed, every day, it will only serve to highlight what we still have to appreciate. We may have destroyed our good name and be the laughing stock in our old community, but we can still lay claim to relative good health, our minds still function more or less and we have enough money for food and shelter. Our job can help us to pulverise the ego and provide round-the-clock opportunities for gratitude.

Our new kind of work should ideally also enable us to access a feeling that, in other circumstances, we would have lost entirely: the sense that we can make a positive difference to others' lives. Of late, we might only have experienced our power to mess everything up. We will have been an exceptional problem to those around us: upsetting friends and family, letting down colleagues, shocking strangers. Our very presence has been offensive to so many. But thanks to a certain sort of job, we can – in a limited way – feel that we are the sort of person that others can call upon for help. It may be a relatively minor intervention, but we can bring water to a cancer patient in a hospice, teach a child how to do their times tables or calm down a suicidal patient in a clinic for troubled teenagers. It really doesn't matter if the job pays very much and we certainly won't care if anyone in the wider world knows that we're doing it; it will offer something infinitely more important than prestige or material reward: a feeling that there's a reason for us to keep existing.

We are used to career services that tend to the needs of the young. What we need is an alternative service specifically geared to the needs of the failed. Such a career service would take stock of our disaster and try to determine our particular areas of competence and interest. Then it would attempt to match us with an urgent societal problem commensurate in scale with our woes.

A supreme example of an inspiring career adjustment in the wake of failure lies in the life of the British Conservative politician and War Secretary John Profumo, who in June 1963 – at the age of 48 and after a hugely successful career in the military and in the senior ranks of government – had to resign after being caught in an affair with a 19-year-old model, Christine Keeler – an affair which had endangered national security and led him to lie to the Prime Minister, the security services and the House of Commons.

A more complete fall from grace had scarcely ever visited a British politician. Profumo had no hope of returning to his previous life. He was a national disgrace and the subject of taunts and mockery. Rotten eggs were thrown at his car. He had let lust blind him to his responsibilities to his family, his party and his country. For a few months he was entirely despondent. Then, in early 1964, seven months after his resignation, Profumo wrote a letter to Walter Birmingham, who ran Toynbee Hall, a centre for disadvantaged people in Whitechapel, one of the most economically depressed parts of East London. Profumo asked if he could possibly be of any help, even perhaps cleaning the toilets (this was a man who had, a year before, held one of the great offices of state). Birmingham had a noble heart and a keen sense of how people could turn their lives around, whether they were kids just out of prison or a disgraced Conservative minister. So he wrote back to Profumo and asked him to come and see him. The letter saved Profumo's life. Suddenly, he had a mission to solve problems far larger and more desperate than his own.

The disgraced politician threw himself into his work. He did everything from cleaning to reforming the management structure of the organisation to raising funds for new initiatives. He became an exemplary employee – never complaining, never alluding to his past and treating everyone with exceptional grace and kindness. His ego had disappeared in the heat of his scandal. All he wished to do was serve. Paradoxically, so well did he serve, so uncomplaining was his approach, so uninterested was he in himself, that his example attracted notice from former friends and enemies in politics. In 1975, after multiple recommendations, he was appointed a Commander of the Order of the British Empire (CBE) in a ceremony at Buckingham Palace. In 1995, Prime Minister Margaret Thatcher held a 70th birthday party at which she sat Profumo next to the Queen. When he died, the lawyer and social reformer Lord Longford remarked that he 'felt more admiration [for Profumo] than [for] all the men I've known in my lifetime'.

A lesson we can all take from Profumo's life is that he wisely did not attempt a 'comeback.' He understood that living quietly for a few years before attempting a return to politics would symbolise a refusal to understand his guilt and a rejection of the opportunities that his

John Profumo (left) with a new minibus for disabled people, for which
he raised the funds, 1998

downfall had afforded for him: to overcome vanity and to open his heart to the needs of ordinary, desperate people that he had hitherto ignored.

After our own downfalls, we should bring some of Profumo's humility and acumen to bear on our destroyed lives. We will need to ask ourselves where our particular passions happen to lie – and how we can connect them up with urgent real-world problems. The answers won't always involve working with poverty in a capital city. Our vocation might be to help blind children to learn to read, or to assist recently arrived refugees, or to tend to elderly prisoners who have been released after serving lengthy terms for sex crimes.

However hard our eventual work will be, it will be doing us the greatest favour: it will show us that we still have a role to play and help us to see that our suffering is neither unique nor uniquely awful. We will hardly need to ask about salaries. Our chief enquiry in interviews will simply be: 'How great is their pain? How can I help?'

Retreat to a hut

One of the most appealing aspects of traditional Chinese culture is the dignified recognition that there might come a time when, for reasons eminently worthy of respect, we will need to leave town and go and live in a hut on a hillside somewhere far away.

In premodern China, it was well understood that politics and public life were a treacherous and unsteady business. Reputations could quickly be made and just as quickly unmade. Rumours might arbitrarily surround a person and render all further public service impossible. One was permanently at risk of falling foul of court factions, of the machinations of enemies, of economic cycles and of military defeats. To expect to lead a long life and not to fail was contrary to any intelligent or subtle understanding of how the universe worked. Good people could – and should – expect to fail, suddenly and definitively.

The question was what might happen next. Chinese culture did not see failure as the end of the story: they were as interested in its consequences as they were in those of success. They understood a need to limit the anxiety that might emerge from a rigidly meritocratic worldview – and the solution they arrived at was the concept of an honourable retreat to a hut. There was room in the Chinese imagination for what were known as *yinshi* (hidden men), *yimin* (disengaged people) and *chushi* (scholars-at-home). These were terms of great affection and esteem for people who had left imperial Beijing and other centres of power, who no longer occupied any prominent place in the social hierarchy, but who still retained a solid claim to honour and respect. These 'disengaged' people could go into the mountains, build themselves small dwellings and then devote themselves to the observation of nature, to the writing of poetry and to the contemplation of the great sacred Buddhist texts. There was understood to be nothing squalid or shameful about their materially modest lives. They had not failed because they were 'bad', but because the way the world was structured meant for constant ebbs and flows of power and influence.

In China's Ming dynasty (1368–1644), government and politics became especially turbulent and prey to arbitrary reversals – and it was at this point in particular that Chinese poets and artists celebrated the idea of a retreat to a hut. In exquisite paintings by great artists like Xiang Shengmo (1597–1658) or Tang Yin (1470–1524)(see overleaf), we find inviting depictions of rural lives – huts that seem to truly compensate for an alienation from the glamour of the city. In valleys shrouded in mist we see yinshi living in beautiful, small wooden houses, often near a stream or by a lake. There are birds overhead, neatly tended gardens and inside the huts, perhaps a scroll with a Buddhist inscription about the futility of all worldly goods or the necessary dissolution of the ego. The once-powerful official is dressed simply but elegantly, usually cross-legged, contemplating the sky or reading a book, fully reconciled to his new existence.

We have made it unbearably hard for ourselves to fail because we have – collectively – been so reluctant to imagine what dignified failure might look like. We quite literally don't know what to do with the failures in our society. We have nowhere for them to go. We don't give them hillsides and huts and Buddhist texts – we expect them to disappear and not spoil our success-oriented vistas.

The Ming Chinese, infinitely wiser in this regard, knew how to budget for failure from the outset. They gave failure a place in their art because they had accepted it as a legitimate occurrence in their lives.

When we fail, we may not need to live in an actual hut. It's what the hut stands for that counts: the acceptance of a life that is simultaneously modest and secluded – as well as dignified and unworthy of contempt. Our hut might be on a hillside in southern Andalusia or in a valley in Sicily or a desert in northern Texas. Or it might just be a place in our minds – a place we can retreat to and enjoy peace without self-hatred.

Top: Xiang Shengmo, *Reading in the Autumn Forest*, 1623
Bottom: Tang Yin, *Thatched Cottage in the Western Mountains*, c. 1499–1520

Our children

We believe – perhaps understandably – that one of the central requirements of being a good parent is to not, at any cost, visibly fail. We undertake enormous efforts to hide our vulnerability to error, foolishness and disaster. We don't tell our children about the tensions at work and our fear of being sacked; we don't reveal how difficult our relationship is and how often we feel defeated and alone; we don't mention to them that we are afflicted by compulsions and addictions that we can't overcome. We hold that a good parent must appear at all times serene, composed, knowledgeable and wise.

These moves are certainly well meant and easy to sympathise with. But *in extremis*, they also do our children a grave injustice. The task of a parent isn't to shelter a child from all failure, but to induct them into the likelihood of mess-ups with reassurance, intelligence and love – to teach them that failure belongs to everyone and that it is possible to be at once kind, clever, idiotic and uncontrolled.

Though we may hope to insulate our children from our failures, the likelihood is that they will sense their presence anyway – but without the help of commentary or honesty. They will sense our depression and anxiety. They will know that something is up over the dinner table. They will have an intuition that there is trouble. The risk is that unless we are open about what is actually happening, they will do what children who are witness to difficulty always do: blame themselves. They will see their depressed and silent father or anxious and irritable mother and come to the most tempting – and in their eyes, logical – conclusion: that they themselves must be wicked, that they must have done something wrong, that they stand in error.

What's more, if we have truly fooled them skilfully, the danger also opens up that our children will start to feel painfully unique in the extent of their own failures and errors. In the context of their lives, they know well enough about their own greed, their own irritability, their own meanness, their own impulsiveness – and yet when they see no correlates for these troubling patterns in the people they admire most, they end up feeling guilty and unique. It seems that their beloved parents don't share in any of their frailties. We are seemingly only ever even-tempered, generous and thoughtful. The child then starts to feel exceptionally bad – in relation to people doing too well at pretending to be completely good.

We do our children an enormous favour when we are able to fail in front of them, unambiguously and with a measure of calming commentary; if we can take them aside and share with them our actual circumstances: that we have been passed over for promotion, that we have stupidly lost some money in an ill-advised scheme, that we're finding it difficult to control our appetites or our temper. They know the problems anyway, in the vague but clever way that children do, but what a relief it will be for them to find an explanation for their intuitions in our own patient words. No child needs a perfect parent; they need a parent who feels real, who can be honest, who doesn't blame them – and who knows how to say sorry when they need to.

Our confession will help them to recognise that their parent is something far better than perfect – they are human, as they themselves are. The candid admission of failure allows a child to extend sympathy and compassion. Their parent isn't angry with them, isn't depressed because of something they did, isn't mean or mysteriously vengeful; they are merely self-disgusted, self-hating and utterly confused.

It might seem like a disorienting concept for a child, but it is far less so than a disguised failure who only serves to alienate them from reality and to deny them the right to truthful explanations. A child would far prefer to know that a parent is in trouble than to fear that the problem lies only with them.

A parent who fails is giving a child a gift of sorts. They allow them to discover that failure is part of every life. They're offering their child something more important than an unblemished childhood: a sincere one, and an induction into how to approach their own darker sides, which they will come across soon enough. By being perfect, a parent is not being perfect; they're making the child feel ashamed of a proclivity to failure that should be recognised as properly universal.

xiv.

Confession

In the Christian tradition, much more so in the olden days than now, it has been customary to head to a small, dark wooden box, about the size of two conjoined phone boxes, and let everything out: what one has done, what one is sorry for and, perhaps, where one remains defiant. After this, a voice would come from the other side of a curtain or grille, reframing the event, placing it within the context of divine love, sympathising but also admonishing – and ending by offering a road to redemption.

In our rush to build a more reasonable, secular world, we have not known how to replace this practice, the function of which has in fact nothing to do with the supernatural but belongs squarely within the requirements of ordinary psychology and civic life. Instead, we have the law, which seeks earthly justice and hands out punishment to transgressors, but proceeds in an implacable way that merely leads most of the accused to deny what they have done and hate those who have asked them to take responsibility. From the legal standpoint, there is no attempt to address the soul of the perpetrator; the idea is chiefly to keep the streets safe and appease the public's hunger for vengeance. How different this is from the Christian approach, which assumes that everyone is a sinner from the outset, insists that everyone routinely errs, and which therefore offers forgiveness for all those courageous enough to examine their consciences and atone with requisite humility.

Instead, the modern world offers up – through the instrument of the media – a version of the old-fashioned pillory, where transgressors are lampooned, where it is automatically assumed that those who did wrong meant to do so and where there is no mercy or sympathy on offer – and therefore, again, no incentive for honesty or confession. Public shaming has – absurdly – become the sole instrument of moral improvement. What would a more psychologically rich processing of error look like? We can imagine the following stages.

— Remember universal sin

In the wake of failure, we are likely to feel intolerably guilty and ashamed, and suicidal thoughts may be at their height. In order to quell these, it is important to stress a fact that is unfashionable, but that has been considered throughout this book: that messing up is an intrinsic feature of our make-up. For Catholics, this proclivity was once classed under the title of 'original sin' (see page 33). According to St Augustine's explanation, we are all the descendants of Adam and Eve – those two early transgressors from God's laws – and therefore indelibly tainted with a temptation to do wrong. Sinning is not some individual freakish occurrence; it is what our species is hard-wired to do.

We don't need to believe in the Biblical truth of this concept to recognise its applicability at moments of crushing self-blame: seeing ourselves as belonging to a species that continually messes up helps to alleviate the devastating shame that can render true atonement impossible. We can chastise ourselves, but before we give way to an impulse to harm ourselves, we should remember that what has befallen us fits into a wider scenario of human frailty. We are still, in the end, bad children – not monsters.

— Acknowledge our psychological compulsions

It is imperative that we allow ourselves to pore over our own histories. The errors we are guilty of have not come from nowhere; we are enmeshed in complicated psychological dynamics that drove them forward. Long ago, we were perhaps bequeathed the legacy of having to please a distant or depressed parent; or we felt invisible and therefore recklessly driven to make exaggerated impressions on strangers; or perhaps our minds were such uncomfortable places to dwell in that we had to find relief in illegal substances or activities.

Knowing where we came from and how we ended up transgressing doesn't in any way excuse us, but it adds context that diminishes suicidal impulses and helps us to face up to our reality. We aren't just brutes or fools; we are wounded and have been for a long time. There will be reasons why we acted as we did – and in a certain mood, we can see the logic of our illness and feel sorry that it should have had such a powerful grip on us.

Unlike what is routinely assumed, we can both take responsibility for our actions and have a measure of broad-minded sympathy for why we perpetrated them. We're not asking to be let off – but we can hope to be understood.

— Apologise

It is not – in general – that we hate apologies; we are merely terrified of articulating one in a situation where it threatens to make everything worse, where it will immediately be attacked for being inadequate and where it will unleash further rage and blame. But – so long as another might listen – how ready we would be to say that we are deeply sorry. Indeed, those in the confessional were apt to reveal so much because they knew their listener had a patient and generous heart.

If only we could be freed from self-hatred and the fear of retribution by a kind ear, we would find ourselves in a place where we could own up to the full panoply of our errors: our selfishness, short-sightedness, greed, lust, gluttony and arrogance. We could try to explain why we acted as we did and why we were cruel, hasty, irrational and without empathy. We could seek a personal meeting with those we had harmed and offer them every restitution we could – while they, alert to their own fragile and erring natures, would understand their role in resolving the cycle of agony through forgiveness.

— Make a plan for atonement

In our secular world, we have grown embarrassingly unimaginative about our strategies for atonement. We can think only of prison, as though to sit in a narrow cell for a few years were truly the best way in which to redeem every ill. But outside of protecting the public from actively violent criminals, there is almost no way in which prison properly helps society to deal with its demons.

Every transgressor – especially those whom modern society never seeks to lock up – should draw up an 'atonement plan', precisely related to the nature of their failure. There we must detail – for the benefit of those we have wronged and perhaps a few curious strangers too – what we intend to contribute going forward in order to rectify the damage we have done, psychological as much as material. There should be offers to explain, to recompense financially, to give up time and to perform what Christians call 'good works'. The Christian of history went on pilgrimages, wrote out passages of the Bible and worked for the sick. We should become comparable experts in the hard work of repair.

— Redemption

In the olden days, the arduous task of forgiveness and redemption was given to God. We didn't have to wrestle with our own ambivalence about letting someone off the hook or our resistance to mapping out paths to making a new start. The secular world makes it harder, but we must overcome our understandable hesitation in believing the promises and sweet words of sinners. We need to take the risk of trusting in the sincerity of those who might have hurt us – in the hope that they will do the same for us when the day comes.

We should never punish or scold without simultaneously offering some kind of path to redemption. No one should fail without being given a chance to atone. We should not hand out unlimited sentences (for prison or social stigmatisation), nor deny anyone the right to reform their characters and do better next year.

We need to do for one another the tasks that we previously entrusted only to angels on the day of judgement. We need to dare to practise divine love.

xv.

Finding Perspective

In normal circumstances, our ingrained impulse is to attempt to grow in importance in our own and others' eyes, to subtly exaggerate our role in events and to magnify the significance of our lives. After failure, however, a very different impulse may come to the fore. Now, what we may most urgently seek is to disappear as definitively as possible. From a practical perspective this might mean exile and a change of name, but there are equally powerful ways to minimise ourselves in an imaginative sense. In the wake of failure we can gain particular relief from moments in which we can reflect on our own brevity, smallness and inconsequence, and in which we can fully and gladly apprehend our complete nothingness – with the help of some of the following sources.

Cosmology

It can be rather dispiriting to digest the fact that our sun, which we naturally take to be a big deal, is in fact only one of 100 billion suns in our galaxy, which in turn lies in a modest corner of a universe made up of a trillion galaxies in which there might be 1,000,000,000,000,000,000,000,000 (or a quadrillion) stars in total. It can be equally terrifying to know that these stars are constantly running out of energy, and that while a few are being born, many are very slowly fading, with our own sun destined to burn out in 7–8 billion years – at which point the Earth, with all its restaurants, headlines, skyscrapers, melodramas, teddy bears, love affairs and tears, will be absorbed back into primal nothingness, and it will be as though nothing had ever disturbed the static silence and darkness of the cosmos.

Once we have failed, though, these thoughts – and other examples of the true scale of time and space – emerge as an unexpected source of supreme therapeutic solace. If our ultimate collective destiny is to be burnt up in a gigantic hydrogen and helium explosion, it may matter slightly less that our reputation is in tatters and that we are being investigated by the authorities. From the vantage point of Icarus, the furthest star ever recorded – more than 9 billion light years from Earth in the region of the supernova Refsdal – very little of what agitates us has any meaning at all. The differences between individual humans fade almost entirely: it hardly matters that we have been sacked while others continue their ascent, that our children are not currently speaking to us, that we have been described as a reprobate and an embarrassment and that we have had to move house in order to escape the hostile stares of neighbours. From the far corners of the universe, one can no longer tell quite who is the fool and who the success story, who is the winner and who deserves to be spat at. Across the 13.8-billion-year history of the universe, our own allotted microsecond of life is as nothing. It doesn't – from the perspective of J0313-1806, the most distant known quasar that holds the furthest supermassive black hole – really matter so much that we are pitiful wretches, unlikely ever to be granted a second chance. Infinite space takes us in its arms and dissolves us into redemptive nonexistence.

Fortunately, we are never too far from such calming thoughts. Every night, so long as the sky is clear, we have one of the finest philosophical lessons ever generated written above us in a faint script of light.

Landscape

There is similar wisdom to be found in those parts of the landscape where nature hints at its true age and force – for example, in the great deserts, by the oceans, at the feet of glaciers or beside the gaping mouths of volcanoes.

We generally pull a tablecloth of a human scale across the Earth and deck it with wheat fields, parks, advertising hoardings and bank towers that help to puff us up and reassure us of our relevance. But occasionally we're reminded of what latecomers we are and how puny our mightiest moments must appear when compared with the forces of nature. We can stand in the Sonoran Desert and contemplate geology that took form 1,200 million years ago, find Palaeozoic shale and limestone that are 240–570 million years old, in which lie fossilised remains of trilobites and brachiopods. We can unearth layers of rhyolite and basalt that were shaped by volcanic explosions 70 million years before we were born, in terrain that was once warm tropical jungle teeming with insects the size of birds.

It isn't just to avoid other humans that we would be wise to make our new post failure home on the edge of a desert. It is because every day, as we take in the landscape around us, we will be eloquently reminded that our erasure is in the end no more tragic or worthy of lament than the disappearance of the Earth's therapsids in the Triassic–Jurassic extinction event 201.3 million years ago (including the adorable *Mastodonsaurus,* who existed blithely and happily for 45.75 million years longer than the pithy 250,000 years that *Homo sapiens* has walked the Earth).

Mastodonsaurus, illustration from
Extinct Monsters and Creatures of Other Days, 1894

In our desert home, we will already be living in an eternity in which we are not included.

History

Comparable relief can also come from the reading of history books, so we would be wise to make these central to our schedules. To abstract us from our circumstances, we can lose ourselves in the history of the Norte Chico civilisation, which formed in what is now Peru in around 3500 BCE, or the exploits of Mesopotamian culture in the Ubaid period (c. 5900–4000 BCE), or the rise and fall of the thirty-one kings of China's Shang dynasty between 1600 and 1046 BCE. We can hold up for our contemplation the battered crowns of forgotten Norse kings, the earrings of long-dead Roman noblewomen or the burial hoard of once-terrifying Mongol leaders.

We are usually taught to read history books in order to discover other peoples and times, but we can do so just as usefully – given our condition – to drive home the message that no peoples and no times ever resist the forces of entropy and oblivion. History, even the most well-recorded kind, is filled with raided tombs, empty caskets, lost books and indecipherable texts. Most of what mattered then doesn't endure; almost all that was once deemed important is trampled underfoot or buried beneath a car park. We can read history as a promise – an advance notice – that we will one day also, thankfully, be forgotten.

Animals

After failure, we should pay a great deal of attention to animals – especially ducks, sheep, cows and squirrels – chiefly because they pay so little attention to us. Even if they are living in close proximity to us, even if they depend on us for their food supplies, most animals are thoroughly uninterested in everything connected with us. They may come over and nibble at some lettuce or take some nuts from our hand, but they have no thought of looking into our eyes. They would as gladly take nourishment from a convicted felon as they would from a prince or a reigning pop star. The sheep chewing lazily by an oak tree have no interest in the latest dramas in our lives, in the slights we have received, in the hopes we have for rehabilitation or in our shame at our misdeeds. We are as featureless and uninteresting to them as a cloud or an escarpment.

This makes animals ideal companions. They show no proclivity to judge and they don't moralise. They generally don't talk. They offer us their presence, but they don't intrude with their thoughts. They won't suggest that they could have done any better in our shoes and they won't be sentimental or passive-aggressive in their words of comfort. They will simply sit beside us for a while, breathing heavily, occasionally burping or farting. And then they will bid us goodbye – perhaps returning to say a downbeat hello the next day.

We may have failed in the world of men; we still have so many interesting afternoons to spend in the company of animals.

xvi.

The Downfall of Oscar Wilde

On Valentine's Day in 1895 at the St James's Theatre in London, the most famous playwright in the English-speaking world at the time, Oscar Wilde, presented his new play, *The Importance of Being Earnest*. The audience was packed with celebrities, aristocrats and famous politicians, eagerly awaiting another triumph from a man universally heralded as a genius. At the end of the performance, there was a standing ovation. Critics adored the play and so did audiences, making it Wilde's fourth major success in only three years.

Yet, only a few short months later, Wilde was bankrupt and about to be imprisoned. His reputation was in tatters and his life ruined beyond repair. It was, as everyone then and now agreed, a tragedy; the swift fall of a great man due to a small but fateful slip.

The story of how Oscar Wilde went from celebrity playwright to prisoner in such a short space of time has much to teach us about disgrace and infamy. We don't have to be similarly lauded to understand that Wilde's poignant tragedy urges us to abandon our normal moralism and have sympathy for those who stray. It calls for us to extend our love not just to those who obviously deserve it, but precisely to those who seem not to. We talk a lot about what a civilised world should be like, but we might put it like this: a civilised world would be one in which Oscar Wilde could have been forgiven – and in which those who make errors of judgement could be treated with high degrees of sympathy and, even, of kindness. It would be a world in which we could remember that good people can at times do bad things – and should not pay an eternal price for them.

Wilde's tragedy began when he was introduced to a beguiling young man named Lord Alfred Douglas. Douglas, known to family and friends as 'Bosie', was extremely handsome, charming and arrogant. He enjoyed gambling, spent money carelessly and was prone to outbursts of anger as well as moments of great intellectual insight.

By 1892, a year after they had met, the two men had fallen profoundly in love. Although Wilde was married with two children, he spent much of his time with Bosie. There was a sixteen-year age gap: Douglas was 24, Wilde 40. They travelled together, stayed in hotels and hosted large dinners for their friends.

Their relationship was tempestuous, but Wilde was ineluctably drawn to the younger man. 'It is really absurd,' he wrote to him in one love letter, 'I can't live without you.' By 1894, the pair were constantly seen together in public and rumours of their love affair had spread as far as Bosie's father, the Marquess of Queensbury. The Marquess was a cruel, aggressive character, known for inventing the 'Queensbury Rules' of amateur boxing. Having decided that Wilde was corrupting his son, he demanded that the pair stop seeing each other. When Wilde refused, Queensbury began to hound him across London, threatening violence against restaurant and hotel managers if they allowed Wilde and Bosie onto the premises. Queensbury booked a seat for the opening night of *The Importance of Being Earnest*. He planned to throw a bouquet of rotting vegetables at Wilde when he took to the stage. When Wilde heard about the stunt, he had him barred from the theatre and Queensbury flew into a rage. He tried to accost Wilde after the performance at the Albemarle Club in Mayfair. When the porters refused to let him in, he left a calling card that publicly accused Wilde of having sex with other men.

Since homosexuality was illegal and deeply frowned upon in Victorian society and its mass media, it was a dangerous accusation. Seeing no end to Queensbury's bullying behaviour, Wilde decided to take legal action. By suing Queensbury for libel, Wilde hoped to clear his name and put an end to the harassment. Friends begged him to drop the case, certain that he would lose, but Bosie insisted that he go ahead with it so that they might be vindicated and be able to live without censorship.

When the trial began, Wilde was confident. He took the stand and gave witty, distracting answers during his cross-examination. Within a few days, however, the tide had turned against him. In the opening speech for the defence, Queensbury's barrister announced that they had several witnesses: young men whom Wilde had entertained in his room at the Savoy Hotel, and who would testify that Wilde had paid them for sex.

It became clear that Queensbury's lawyers had hired private detectives to uncover an uncomfortable truth: that both Wilde and Bosie had hired male prostitutes. Some had even blackmailed Wilde in the past, successfully extorting money from him in return for their silence. The trial was hopeless, and Wilde withdrew his case, but events had spiralled beyond his control. Queensbury's lawyers forwarded their evidence to the Director of Public Prosecutions and Wilde was soon arrested on charges of gross indecency. The legal costs left him bankrupt and theatres were forced to abandon his plays.

Wilde's criminal trial began at the Old Bailey on 26th April 1895. He faced twenty-five charges, all of which surrounded his sexual relationships with younger men. Wilde continued to deny the allegations and the jury could not reach a verdict, but when the prosecution was allowed to try Wilde a second time, he was eventually found guilty. It was rumoured that the then prime minister, Archibald Primrose, 5th Earl of Rosebery, had also had an affair with one of Queensbury's sons and so pushed for Wilde to be convicted in order to keep his own secret hidden. The judge said at his sentencing, 'It is the worst case I have ever tried. ... I shall pass the severest sentence that the law allows. In my judgment it is totally inadequate for such a case as this.'

Wilde was sentenced to two years of hard labour. Inmates in London's Pentonville Prison, where he was sent, spent six hours a day walking on a heavy treadmill or untangling old rope using their hands and knees. For someone from Wilde's luxurious background, it was an impossible hardship. His bed was a hard plank, which made it difficult to fall asleep. Prisoners were kept alone in their cells and barred from talking to one another. He suffered from dysentery and became physically very frail.

After six months, Wilde was transferred to Reading Gaol. As he stood on the central platform of Clapham Junction, with handcuffs around his wrists, passers-by began to recognise the celebrity playwright. They laughed and mocked. Some even spat at him. 'For half an hour I stood there,' he wrote afterwards, 'in the grey November rain surrounded by a jeering mob. For a year after that was done to me, I wept every day at the same hour and for the same space of time.'

During his last year in prison, he wrote an anguished essay, *De Profundis*: 'I, once a lord of language, have no words in which to express my anguish and my shame. ... Terrible as was what the world did to me, what I did to myself was far more terrible still. ... The gods had given me almost everything. But I let myself be lured into long spells of senseless and sensual ease. ... I allowed pleasure to dominate me. I ended in horrible disgrace. There is only one thing for me now, absolute humility. ... I have lain in prison for nearly two years. ... I have passed through every possible mood of suffering. ... The only people I would care to be with now are artists and people who have suffered: those who know what beauty is, and those who know what sorrow is: nobody else interests me.'

In May 1897, Wilde was finally released. He set sail for Dieppe in France the very same day. His wife, Constance, had changed her name and moved abroad with their two sons, Vyvyan (now 11) and Cyril (12). Wilde would never see his children again; he missed them every day. Constance agreed to send him money on the condition that he end his relationship with Bosie, but only a few months later the pair reunited and the money stopped. They moved to Naples and Wilde began using the name Sebastian Melmoth, inspired by the great Christian martyr St Sebastian and a character from a Gothic novel, *Melmoth the Wanderer*, who had sold his soul to the devil.

Wilde and Bosie hoped to find privacy abroad, but the scandal seemed to follow them wherever they went. English patrons recognised them in hotels and demanded they be turned away. After Constance stopped sending money, Bosie's mother offered to pay their debts if he returned home and the pair once again parted ways. Scorned by many of his former friends, Wilde moved to Paris, where he lived in relative poverty. He spent most of his time and money in bars and cafes, borrowing funds whenever he could and drinking heavily. His weight ballooned and his conversation dragged. He was slowly inebriating himself to death. When a friend suggested he try to write another comic play, he replied: 'I have lost the mainspring of life and art ... I have pleasures, and passions, but the joy of life is gone.'

Wilde's final piece of writing, a poem entitled 'The Ballad of Reading Gaol', was published in 1898. The author's name was listed as 'C.3.3.' – Wilde's cell block and cell number from his time in the prison. Towards the end of 1900, Wilde developed meningitis and became gravely ill. A Catholic priest visited his hotel and baptised him into the church. He died the following day at the age of 46.

More than a century later, in 2017, a law was passed to exonerate those who had been convicted due to their sexuality and Oscar Wilde received an official pardon from the UK government. 'It is hugely important,' declared a government minister, 'that we pardon people convicted of historical sexual offences who would be innocent of any crime today.'

Our society has become generous towards Wilde's specific behaviour – but it remains intransigently moralistic towards a huge number of other errors and transgressions; we need only read the newspaper to be reminded of the cruelty. The crowd continues to enjoy watching people be disgraced (to appease some unhappiness in their own hearts), refusing to see the humanity in those whom it likes to call 'monsters'. Many of us would want to reach out across the ages to comfort and befriend Oscar Wilde. It's a touching hope, but this feeling would be better employed in extending love and sympathy to all those figures who are right now facing ruin and disgrace, who cry out for our love and sympathy and beg us not to judge them too harshly or spit on them too callously on their way to jail. That would be true civilisation and a world in which Wilde's horrifying downfall had not been in vain.

xvii.

A New Attitude

Failure does not only strip us of 'things' – friends, status, money, respect. It can also bequeath us a distinctive outlook on life; a philosophy forged in the turmoil of failure, with unexpected positive attributes. We can expect some of the following character traits to be strengthened in those who have learnt to fail well.

Gallows humour

After we experience failure, we may start to laugh more often – not in a jolly, light-hearted kind of way, but from a humour based on the tragic and dark gulf between how we would want things to be and how they have turned out. We'll joke about despair and terror: we'll become practitioners of 'gallows humour'. Mostly, the jokes we make will be at our own expense. There will be so much in our lives that people think is too sad to mention: that almost all our friends have ditched us, that our name is all over the internet, that our children don't speak to us. The normal response in these cases is usually to skirt the issue. One can fall prey to the vain superstition that if one doesn't bring up an unfortunate fact, it might just fade away of its own accord. But not mentioning sadness is also what lets it win its sapping victories over us. We suffocate from timidity around our griefs. The strategy of gallows humour is different; it is usefully and gloriously defiant. It insists on mentioning the grim aspects of life and our situations, asserting control over them through mordant, dry commentary. In the Middle Ages, a tradition began in which the condemned, standing on the scaffold before their demise, would turn to the crowd and make a witticism about their situation. Sigmund Freud recounts a man being led out to be hung at dawn saying, 'Well, the day is certainly starting well.' Gallows humour is not squeamish about looking bleakness straight in the eye. Rather than being slowly gnawed at by sideways glances at the truth, the gallows humourist insists that they will not be silenced by it – they roll their sleeves up and grab it tenaciously.

In these circumstances, laughter becomes a kind of grateful relief at witnessing our most shameful secrets handled with such reassuringly confident *sangfroid*. We might cheerfully exclaim: 'In the days when I wasn't thought worse than Adolf H. ...' or, 'Being alive is still marginally better than being dead, but it's a close-run thing ...' Gallows humour resists the temptation to complain earnestly. By frankly referring to something appalling, we can bolster our capacity not to be crushed by it. We don't need to be great comics to generate gallows humour. The technique follows a simple pattern: we just need to head directly for the saddest, most taboo sides of our failed lives, remain utterly unflinching in front of them – and deliver understated, breezy, unruffled responses. Gallows humour edges the worst facts of our lives into a zone of bearable conversation. It allows us to joke about what we could otherwise never say straight out. It is a technique to stop us being destroyed by silence.

Kindness

The most common reason why people are unkind is that they cannot imagine how they might end up suffering from certain ills: they can't picture themselves becoming homeless, losing their temper, saying something idiotic online or getting into trouble over sex. Because of this, they naturally aren't in a position to extend sympathy to those who have failed in these areas; those people must simply be idiots or reprobates – human in a technical sense, but not creatures with any humanity worth honouring. The moralists who think this way aren't so much unkind as unimaginative. Experience of failure offers a crash course in how decent people (that is, all of us from a sufficient distance) might end up in an appalling place – a lesson that becomes applicable across all areas of mishap. Once we have failed, we can feel pain from the inside. Suffering of all kinds becomes our area of expertise; all distress becomes relatable (how unkind are people who have been happy all their lives). We can picture just what it might be like to have a painful hip as a 90-year-old or to have been told off for eating too many sweets as a 4-year-old – even to be a sparrow that has lost its way home or a squirrel longing for nuts in midwinter. When we read the paper, every unfortunate 'cheater' or 'reject' is someone whose story we can understand and empathise with. We have become kind not out of some superhuman goodness: we just want, for our own sake, to spare everyone we encounter a modicum of the pain we have had to suffer. Our kindness is solidly grounded in self-interest: it hurts us to see someone else in pain.

Gratitude

At one time, we might have had plans for happiness on an epic scale: we might have wanted to be happy 'forever'. Now we are satisfied if no further disaster strikes us before nightfall. We might once have sought out ever-increasing fame and power. Now we have been inducted into how quickly things can fall apart and won't take a quiet day for granted ever again. As newly failed beings, we may turn into people with an acute eye for small pleasures: a lemon on a windowsill, some clouds silhouetted by the evening sun, a fig, a piece of chocolate, a hot bath, a chat with a funny friend. The horizon shrinks: one comfortable lunch is something to celebrate. An afternoon in which we have not been visited by searing regrets is a triumph. It's a massive achievement not to think of killing oneself for an entire weekend. We take it a day at a time.

Humility

One thing that failure strips us of is a feeling that we might be 'good' people. This might indicate that we must therefore be 'bad', but the reality is more complicated. Ironically, people who are genuinely good – people who know about kindness, patience, forgiveness, compromise, apology and gentleness – always suspect that they aren't very good. It seems one cannot both be a good person and at the same time feel blameless or pure inside. Goodness is, one might say, the unique consequence of a keen and ongoing awareness of one's capacity to be bad – that is, to be thoughtless, foolish, cruel, self-righteous and ignorant of the legitimate needs of others. Only on the basis of a perpetual, vigilant impression that one hasn't got the right to judge oneself above suspicion does one come anywhere near the ethical high standard that merits the title of 'good'. The price of being genuinely good is the constant idea that one might be a monster – combined with a fundamental hesitation about labelling anyone else monstrous. A guilty conscience is the bedrock of virtue – and all this comes easily to the failed.

Generally, it never occurs to the most difficult or dangerous people on the planet that they might be lacking. Their sickness is to locate evil always firmly outside of themselves: it's invariably the 'others' who are to blame, the others who are cruel, sinful, lacking in judgement and mistaken. Their job is to take these impure people down and correct their evils in the fire of their own righteousness. The failed don't go in for this. Their sense of uncleanliness is an insurance policy against further evil. It is a grim paradox, therefore, that some of the worst deeds that humans have ever been guilty of have been carried out by people with an easy conscience; people who felt they were definitely on the side of angels, people who were entirely sure that they had justice in hand. What unites the people who report their neighbours to the secret police, the crowds who burn their victims at stakes while dancing around their agonised bodies, the government officials who set up purification camps and the nations that wipe out their enemies with special barbarism is their consistent and overwhelming sense that they are doing the right thing – in the eyes of God, history or truth. When trying to understand why people do evil things, we should never start from the position that they understood them as evil; they carried out their nastiness cocksure that they were paragons. An impassioned feeling of being the instrument of justice has been at the heart of humanity's most appallingly unkind moments. The truly kind ones among us always readily forgive because they know how much in them needs to be forgiven.

xviii.

A Utopian Commune

Modern society tends to offer us two models for our living arrangements: we can either be alone or with a romantic partner. The drawbacks of both options are well known. The first has a habit of leaving us feeling abandoned, the second stifled and restless. We're in danger of either longing for company or wishing that we weren't stuck expecting one other person to fulfil all our emotional and practical needs – and, with even the best intentions, generally failing to do so.

When life is going well enough in other areas, the frustrations are almost bearable. But when everything has been lost, desperation may inspire us to try to find something that can shore us up. This is when an unfamiliar option may start to sound oddly appealing: to live communally in close proximity to other people who have failed.

A community of failed people promises to solve the problems of both loneliness and judgement. In such a place, we will be surrounded by others, but others who will not moralise, sneer or cut us dead. We will be in a 'family' bonded by a vital glue: our joint experience of condemnation and shame.

The failure doesn't have to be identical. Maybe one person ran off with some money, another was in a sex scandal and a third lost their job because of their problem with anxiety. What will unite this diverse set of characters is that they all know the toll of having to live in a society where, even if they don't mean to, others constantly enforce the message that they are strange, rare, pitiable or devilish.

In an ideal community of the failed, life would feel lighter and more liberated because there would be no need to interact with harsh witnesses every day. Chores and routine tasks could be shared out in common: there would be failed people doing the cooking and failed people taking care of the laundry; failed people tending to the vegetable garden and failed people repairing the roof after a storm. It might take place in a simple but beautiful house somewhere out in nature, very far from other people, with the ability to live cheaply and self-sufficiently.

One could hope for an atmosphere of vivid kindness, because everyone in the group would be so familiar with the ravages of self-disgust. Members would encourage one another to keep going, not to lapse into despair and to have faith that black moods will pass. There would be moments of joint confession and atonement.

Collectively, we've been good at dreaming up where cheerful, beautiful people should go. Resorts the world over lend a sense of community to buoyant families and ardent lovers. We know, too, how to lock up people in terrifying prisons and throw away the keys. What we haven't yet found our way to is the building of communities for people who have failed – for those who have surrendered their pride, who are no longer interested in one-upmanship, who are profoundly aware of their flaws and are committed to battling them ... a community of those who recognise that the kindness of others stands as the central reason to remain alive.

In this community, we would not be able to erase our failures, but we would be able to attenuate a great many of their secondary, aggravating characteristics. We would have ruined our lives without losing all experience of kindness and companionship.

xix.

Losers as Winners

Our society has an advanced tendency to label certain people as 'winners' and others – logically enough – 'losers'. Aside from the evident meanness of this categorisation, the underlying problem with it is the suggestion that life might be a unitary, singular race, at the conclusion to which one could neatly rank all the competitors from highest to lowest.

The more confusing and complex truth is that life is really made up of a number of races that unfold simultaneously over very different terrain and with different sorts of cups and medals in view. There are races for money, fame and prestige, of course – and these attract many spectators and, in some social circles, the bulk of the coverage. But there are also races that measure other kinds of prowess worth venerating. There is a race for who can remain calmest in the face of frustration. There is a race for who can be kindest to children. There is a race measuring how gifted someone is at friendship. There are races focused on how attentive someone is to the evening sky or how good they are at deriving pleasure from autumn fruits.

Despite our enthusiasm for sorting competitors into neat ranks, a striking fact about the multi-race event of life is, quite simply, that no one is ever able to be the winner in every competition available. Furthermore, prowess in one kind of race can militate against one's chances of success in others. Winning at being ruthlessly successful in business seems not – for example – generally to go hand in hand with ability in the race to appreciate the sky or find pleasure in figs. Equally, those who are terrific at gaining fame may be hampered when it comes to the race that measures ability to be patient around thoughtful but under-confident 3-year-olds.

We cannot, it seems, be winners at everything. Those who appear to be carrying off all the prizes and who are lauded as the super-human athletes of life cannot, on closer examination, really be triumphing across the board. They are bound to be making a deep mess of some of the less familiar or prestigious races they are entered in for; in certain corners of the stadium, they'll be falling over, tripping up, complaining loudly about track conditions and, perhaps, sourly denigrating the whole event as useless and not worth participating in.

If one cannot be a winner at everything, it follows that one cannot be a loser at everything either. When we have failed in certain races in the milliathlon of life, we retain ample opportunities to train and develop our strength to win in others. We may never again be able to compete in the race for fame, honour or money, but it's still entirely open to us to compete in the race for kindness, friendship and forgiveness. We may even win in the not insignificant races for enjoying one's own company or sleeping very soundly and without anxiety for many hours.

There is no such thing as a winner or a loser, per se. There is only a person who has won in some areas and messed up in others. And, to go deeper, someone whose talent at winning in one sort of race means they must naturally and almost inevitably mess up in alternatives – and vice versa.

We never fail at life itself. When we mess up in worldly areas and feel dejected and isolated, the universe is just giving us an exceptional chance to begin the training that will one day mean we become star athletes in other less well-known but hugely important races – races about keeping a sense of humour, showing gratitude, forgiving, appreciating, letting go and making do. These are the noble tracks on which those who have 'failed' can finally, properly and redemptively learn to 'win'.

xx.

Time

When it's just happened, our failure hurts so much because the memory of what we have lost is so vivid. We remember what it was like the previous summer – when we could still look forward to a prosperous future, when we were still being invited out, when we had some money and could sleep. During this time, we are continually tortured by the difference between what is and what might have been. If only we had been more careful with the document, if only we had listened to reason, if only we hadn't been so greedy, thoughtless, arrogant, lustful or vain ...

But the more the situation settles, the more we start to appreciate – with mature darkness – that there were some rather weighty reasons why things unfolded as they did. We were greedy, thoughtless, arrogant, lustful or vain not by random chance, but for reasons that run deep in our characters. We may not like the flowers that emerged, but the roots of these plants run many metres down and would almost certainly have manifested themselves somewhere, at some point, perhaps in even less propitious ways.

What seems to have happened by – we initially think – a totally avoidable piece of ill luck emerges over time as a phenomenon with a firm, albeit grim, logic. Failure wasn't merely a coincidence or happenstance. The constituents of failure are as much part of us as the imprints of our fingers. We can't lean across to an adjoining table and wish we could have this bit of a more accomplished friend's life or that portion of a stranger's good fortune. We have to pay allegiance to who we actually are – in all zones of life, of which failure is in the end just one.

We will also, fortunately, start to forget. The alternative narrative in which we did not fail will grow ever more distant. We won't remember the way that the next year was supposed to go. We will forget what it was like to go to parties. We won't recognise the names of our enemies. As the months and years pass, what should not have happened will turn into what had to happen.

We will have had to fail – and then we will have learnt – in other areas, remarkably, in ways we had never expected and that still feel alien and impossible now – how to win.

Part II:

The Fear of Failure

i.

Failure Imagined

We have been looking at how to understand and cope with actual failure: disgrace, scandal, bankruptcy, unemployment, mental illness, family separation, marital breakdown ...

However, in considering the subject, we also need to acknowledge a curious phenomenon: that cases of actual failure only comprise a portion – and perhaps the smaller portion – of the nightmare that the topic of failure plunges us into. Most of the failure that ails us hasn't happened yet – and may never. It is apprehended failure: a failure of what might occur; a feverish deduction from our worst forebodings. We have spent valuable time torturing ourselves with scenarios that didn't come to pass. We have ruined some of the best days of our lives ruminating on catastrophes that in the end left us untouched. We have worried about the end of relationships that continued, we have panicked about money that didn't run out, we have feared reputational ruin that didn't visit us. We have wasted days by the sea on beautiful islands or in exciting foreign cities because in our minds, we were not able to be present at all, because we were rigid with terror, fearing the call of a journalist, a pained apology from a lover, an email from our boss, the collapse of our minds ... We may have spent our lives outwardly free, while crouching in a cage of apprehension of our own making.

The fear of failure is every bit as serious and painful as failure itself. Just because an incident doesn't happen in the three-dimensional world doesn't mean that we can skirt its ravages. A calamity that is endlessly anticipated is in its way every bit as awful as a calamity that actually unfolds – with the added problem that fears tend to go on far longer than 'real' incidents. We might spend three decades ruminating on a fear of something that, if it really occurred, might only spoil a few years. Worries can be yet more destructive than the events they apprehend.

There are two ways of interpreting our fears of failure: that they are entirely made up and a consequence of inner emotional turmoil, or that they have some connection to true dangers but are wildly overblown and would be survivable even if they came to pass. Both cases deserve compassion and curiosity – as well as thorough responses and coping strategies.

What follows is a consideration of the subject, which takes anticipated failure every bit as seriously as its real-world cousin – and which proposes that, just like it, it can eventually be endured and borne ...

and even leave us alone every now and then to enjoy the view and a little more of our brief and precious lives.

ii.

Fear and Soothing

The inner life of a properly fearful person is so tormented that an ordinary day is able to serve up more occasions for terror and trepidation than would, for most of us, a rafting trip down one of the world's angriest rapids. On the outside, the fearful person may be doing nothing more remarkable than looking after a home or going to an office, but this tells us nothing about the scale of the challenges that they will be facing internally.

From the moment they wake up, they will be haunted by a succession of the cruelest 'what ifs'. What if an email has arrived overnight detailing news of an illness or scandal? What if the newspaper carries a story about an event that might destroy their livelihood? What if their partner's unusually severe or distracted manner is the first sign of a problem that ends in separation? What if the slight pain behind the eyes is the beginning of mental degeneration? What if they forgot to do something at work, which results in ruin? The questions never stop and nor does the worried person's inability to find any satisfying and calming answers to them. Their worries flap and bang in the winds of the mind all day and night like a badly fastened shutter in a winter storm.

The fearful person doesn't have a more frightening life than anyone else; they just lack the resources to extinguish the embers of worry that befall all of us in the course of an average day. At every turn, they end up with a major conflagration on their hands. The party they have to go to, the meeting they are attending, the letter they have to open, the social media feed they scroll through – each of these delivers yet another electric bolt of horror into their system.

How did life get to be so frightening for them? To understand this, we should travel far back in time and imagine a baby in the middle of the night. The room is dark, and the baby is hungry and wet right through. There is a terrible pain in their stomach and a tingly cold feeling all around their waist and their legs. Unable to work out what is wrong and without any means of altering it, the baby starts to scream, then ever louder, with all the desperation and strength in their young lungs; fast, panicky screams, begging for deliverance and assistance from multiple sources of pain that will not let up. Finally, after what felt like an age, but could in reality have been only a minute or two, a light comes on and, like a piece of supernatural intervention, the friendliest face in the world appears, illuminated from behind, with a gentle smile and encouraging eyes, and says: 'Now, now, what seems to be the matter? It looks like poppet might want a feed and maybe a new nappy ...' The words don't make any sense, but what happens next certainly does: the baby is lifted out of their cot, carefully changed, warmed and then settled at the breast, where they feed on the most satisfying and delicious meal that culinary art has ever produced, listening – in the background, alongside its own sucking noises – to the soft rhythm of a heart whose reassuring beats it remembers so well from the womb.

From such experiences, repeated over many months, the baby learns to develop a vital trust in life. There may be pain and there might be fear, but these aren't eternal punishments. There are solutions to even the greatest terrors. A larger person can come along and make sense of the distress. The world doesn't have to be filled with unending torment.

Later, if the young person's luck holds, similar forms of alleviation will continue – when, for example, Teddy loses its leg, when a bottle falls off the table and shatters across the kitchen floor, when another child comes and steals a toy, when Granny is ill, when their bike crashes into a tree, when it's the first day at school ... At all such moments, a kindly adult is on hand to reassure, to contextualise, to explain, to offer sympathy, to look forward to better times and to plot alternative ways forward.

Through such manoeuvres, the child picks up the skill of soothing. Later on, when they have graduated, when they're out in the world, when they have love affairs and dependents and responsibilities at work, the lessons of the early days will still reverberate and offer a toolkit with which upsets and reversals can be faced. There may be some genuinely thorny problems, but they don't have to be a catastrophe; this won't be the end. The robust person understands that there are a great many steps between a danger sign and collapse. With one side of them acting as parent to the other, they can tell themselves, 'We may have loved them very much, but we will find others and have many good friends to see in the meanwhile,' or 'The criticism was very unfair and a little damaging, but we don't need everyone to like us and have just enough support to continue as we are.'

Unfortunately, however, there are many less privileged people who have been gifted no such pacifying resources in their early lives. Perhaps when they screamed in the early hours, no adult came – or the one who did was as panicked as they were or seemed to be furious to be woken up at such an hour. Maybe the adult who came made the baby feel wicked for being so angry or was frightened by the intensity of the little one's needs. Later on, it's likely there was no easy recovery from a broken toy or a smashed bottle. Every graze generated an insuperable drama; every problematic moment at school was a cause of lasting commotion. From such experiences, there came a grave shortfall in the capacity for self-soothing. The muscle of the mind that might otherwise have argued the case for calm, forgiveness, perspective and compassion lacked any training. And therefore, there could only ever be a few short steps between a small reversal and a significant crisis: there could be no such thing as an insignificant or manageable problem. There could only ever be panic and cataclysm.

It may help us to understand our own fragilities to describe them as stemming from an inability to self-soothe. We are not wicked or dumb; we simply never learnt how to calm ourselves down because, long ago, no one *else* knew how to calm us down. We acquired lessons not in minimising the impact of reversals but in aggrandising minor misfortunes. We unwittingly became world experts in alarm.

With this sad knowledge painfully absorbed and mourned, we may be in a better position to learn – many decades later than we should – how to begin to utter a few calming affirmations in our minds. We can start to hunt out with greater vigour the sort of voices that should have been absorbed by our 3-month-old selves: the tranquillising tones of certain friends and authors, psychotherapists or lovers. The adult side of us can learn to play parent to a younger and more defenceless inner one. We can, metaphorically, stroke our own hair, wipe away our own tears – and feel sad that this form of nurture never came our way spontaneously in the early, jittery days.

In the process we will learn that we don't live in an exceptionally dangerous world; we simply happen to have endured an exceptionally unsoothing past.

iii.

Fear and Self-hatred

In trying to discover the origins of fear, we may need to look in a slightly unobvious place: not in the purported content of our concerns, but instead (a topic we may be very reluctant to consider) in how we feel about ourselves. It may be that certain kinds of worries are, in the end, driven not so much by anything especially alarming in the world as by a compulsive need to find ourselves awful. Our fears may be a leading symptom of self-hatred.

Imagine someone at an airport heading out for a much-deserved and long-anticipated holiday. As they make their way through the check-in process, they start to become increasingly fearful that in their absence, they will be undermined by colleagues and eventually sacked. The thought doesn't leave them alone and by the time they reach their destination, they are certain that their career is over.

Or, imagine someone in the early stages of a hugely satisfying love affair. Their new partner is kind, thoughtful and very funny. But one evening, when this partner is out with friends, the fearful person becomes sure that they are being cheated on; the partner must have met someone else and love is about to fail for them once again.

If we drill into our core, it becomes apparent that many worries are essentially efficient ways of beating ourselves up and of doubting whether we are good enough to deserve anything satisfying and desirable. By worrying, we are finding a highly efficient way of depriving ourselves of the right to be content. Somewhere inside our worried mind is a sense of being an unworthy person. Our fears are plugged into boundless subterranean stores of self-hatred.

If our starting position is one of self-hatred, then we shouldn't be surprised if we are never able to have a relaxing holiday or a mutually joyful love affair. Sadly, however, our minds don't come clean about their workings; they don't draw our attention to their perverse logic. Fears like to insist that they only concern themselves: the bungled email, the rumour, the missed call ... But to be so certain that things are about to go wrong for us, at some point in our personal evolution we must have been given a sense that we were unworthy and shameful. We insist that bad things will happen to us because surely bad things must happen to bad people.

This analysis implies that we should stop taking our worries at face value; rather than ruminating without end on each example, we should shift towards a different and more salient topic – we should replace our anxious questions with a single, bolder sideways enquiry:

'Why can't I be kinder to myself?' The most effective way to calm down might be to try to address our feelings of unworthiness rather than seek reassurance for our panic.

We don't so much have fears to face – we have a deficit of self-love to make up. If we can find a way to feel more loveable, we might discover that the world also feels less fearsome.

iv.

Trauma and Fearfulness

The core reason why many of us are more fearful than we should be is that we are – unbeknownst to ourselves – wandering through our lives with a huge burden of unresolved and unobserved *trauma*.

A trauma is not merely a terrible event (though it is very much that too); it is a terrible event that has not been adequately processed, understood and unpicked and that has – through neglect – been able to cast a long and undeserved shadow over huge areas of experience. Many of our greatest fears have nothing at all to do with actual dangers in the here and now; they are the legacy of traumas that we have lacked the wherewithal to be able to trace back to their origins, to localise and to neutralise.

The concept of trauma was first observed in military contexts. Let us imagine a young man, in bed one night in a country torn apart by civil war. He hears a car alarm, followed, a few seconds later, by a huge explosion. The neighbourhood is destroyed and several members of his family are killed. He is devastated, but under pressure to continue with his life, is unable to reflect adequately or properly to mourn what has happened; he is forced to move on from a dreadful experience with fateful haste and lack of emotional assimilation. And yet the unattended memory of bloodshed, chaos and loss doesn't disappear. Instead, it curdles into an unknown interior presence we call trauma – which means that in the years and decades ahead, even in the most peaceful circumstances, whenever he hears a car alarm or indeed any high-pitched sound (that of an elevator's ping, for example) he will be mysteriously thrown back into the original panic, as if 1,000 tons of TNT were about to explode once again.

However appalling this can be, psychologists have learnt that trauma can as easily be acquired in ostensibly peaceful circumstances. We don't need to have been through a war to be traumatised in multiple ways.

Imagine a 6-year-old child who makes an error in a maths exam and takes the news home; suddenly, her father – who drinks too much and might be battling depression and paranoia – flies into a rage, shouts at her, smashes a glass and slams the kitchen door. From the perspective of a 6-year-old, it feels like the world is ending. There is no way to make sense of the moment – beyond taking responsibility for it, and as a result feeling like a terrible human being. From this, a trauma develops, this one centred around making mistakes. It seems to the young girl that every slip threatens to unleash an explosion in others. Far into adulthood, every time there is a risk of an error, a terror arises in her that someone else will become dementedly furious. Everyone becomes terrifying because the one person in particular who was so scary hasn't been thought about and reckoned with in memory.

Alternatively, we might imagine a little boy who is looked after by a very loving but very fragile single mother, who is prudish and scared of masculinity. The boy feels her disapproval and grows acutely guilty about his own more boisterous, vital dimensions. From this, he eventually develops a trauma around his sexual feelings; a part of him believes that to be sexual is to upset women – and therefore, even when he is with women who are keen on intimacy with him, he finds himself unable to feel excited or potent and always, for reasons he doesn't understand, moves to end the relationship. Every woman is imagined as disgusted with sex because one important woman in his formative years was thought to have been.

In all such cases, the solution is to get a better sense of the specific incidents in the past that have generated difficulties in order to unhook the mind from its expectations. The clue that we are dealing with a trauma – rather than any sort of justified fear – lies in the scale and intensity of feelings that descend in conditions when there is no objective rationale for them: it's peacetime, a man is kind, a woman is full of desire ... and yet still there is terror, still there is self-disgust, still there is shame. We know then that we are dealing not with 'silliness' or 'madness' or indeed genuine danger, but with an unprocessed incident from the past casting a debilitating shadow on a more innocent present.

As traumatised people, the memory of the original incident is within us, but our conscious minds swerve away from the possibility of engaging with it and neutralising it through rational examination. Unable to mourn or decipher the event, much of life becomes mournful and not worth living. At the same time, the trauma breeds symptoms and neuroses that we cannot trace back to their founding moment – we forget why we are so scared, we just know that there are risks everywhere. A trauma is an agony that the conscious mind has lacked the support and resources to process – at the cost of our ability to love, to be free and to think creatively.

Yet if we can finally feel comfortable and safe enough to dare to look back, we'll be able to see the traumatising moment for what it was, outside of our original panic and our youthful or illogical conclusions (that it was our fault, that we did something wrong, that we are sinful). Liberating ourselves will mean understanding the specific, local and relatively unique features of what has traumatised us, and then growing aware of how our minds have multiplied and universalised the difficulty, in part to protect us from an encounter that was once too difficult to grapple with.

We will realise that it was one bomb that exploded and destroyed the neighbourhood – and that however dreadful this might have been, there is no reason for all high-pitched noises to terrify us. Similarly, it was one father who screamed at us for making a mistake when we were tiny – and not everyone who is in authority threatens to annihilate us in adulthood. Or it was one particular woman who made us feel that our sexuality was unacceptable, and so we should not assume that all women are revolted by us.

Situations will continue to be frightening so long as individual incidents have not been understood and thought through with kindness and imagination. By properly gripping an establishing event in the claws of our rational adult mind and stripping it of its mystery, we will be able to repatriate fearful emotions – and render the world less unnerving than it presently seems. Life as a whole doesn't have to be so terrifying, once we understand the bits of it that truly were.

V.

Fear and Money

In many circles, those who work far more than they strictly need to and who strive with exceptional energy to accumulate as much money as possible are likely to be sneered at and lightly mocked. They may be dismissed as 'workaholics' and categorised as 'greedy'.

However, the story gets more complicated if we allow ourselves to enter imaginatively into their experiences (and perhaps compare them to our own). We may return to the office earlier than we need to, and be at our desk every weekend, because idleness makes us intensely uncomfortable. A feeling of eeriness and dread tends to descend on holidays, yet when we are racing against a self-imposed deadline, when every hour is timetabled for the next six months, we feel exhausted but also harnessed and directed. We have a plan that appears to guide and protect us. Similarly, we know we may not need all the money we are saving up and we understand there is no urgent necessity to go on yet another exhausting business trip, but with every large invoice we send out, we anticipate a feeling of calm and well-being.

In other words, beneath the apparent 'workaholism' and 'greed', something more interesting and vulnerable is stirring: we are on a search for safety. We tire ourselves building up financial reserves because this promises to deliver us a sense of assurance that we long for with an intensity we may not quite understand. We're not rapacious at all; we just feel in danger. Those who are particularly materially acquisitive are not vainer than the rest of us; they are simply far more frightened.

At a primal, unconscious level, money promises to be the conclusive answer to panic. With sufficient wealth, we sincerely believe that we can be at peace. We won't have to be unnerved by people ever again, we won't need to be surprised and terrified.

Unfortunately, there is just enough truth in the longing to keep it alive for a lifetime. Money can – of course – on occasion spare us humiliation and difficulty. But its power is ultimately limited and always surpassed by our inner terror. The entrenched fear we wrestle with has a stubborn habit of enduring long after our most hopeful financial targets have been met. We might accumulate 100 or 500 million pounds and still – agonisingly – not be at peace. We may retire to a villa surrounded by a high wall patrolled by a private security firm and be sitting by an Olympic-sized pool sipping on an elderflower cordial, served to us by a kind and deferential servant, *and still not feel safe.* Four decades of constant labour may find us in a mansion in which we remain wracked by anxiety.

This paradox can only be explained by drilling into the roots of our original fear. As with most of our fears, an exorbitant longing for wealth is almost always generated by an experience of unmanageable let-down and humiliation in early life. People don't acquire a craving for superabundant riches until – and unless – they suffer a catastrophe in their formative years that they are unable to process and make sense of. Wealth becomes one of the primary compensatory fantasies in cases of unmanageable emotional loss; with wealth there promises to be an end to the aching and the self-doubt, the anxiety and the despair. With wealth, there will never again be a misfortune that cannot be mastered.

Instead of blindly pursuing wealth, we should strive to remember, and to overcome, the original trauma that we suffered at the hands of others. We must keep in mind that we work harder than most because we were let down more than most – in a way that we have avoided focusing on all our adult lives. We need to find the sympathetic environment in which we can travel back in time to revisit our primal sorrow: the father who abandoned us, the mother who was too busy to care for us, the grandmother who mocked us. None of our financial skills will serve any useful purpose in terms of reducing panic until we can reconnect with the frightened little child we once were – and bring them the understanding and emotional reassurance they lacked. That will make us feel safe in a way no mansion ever can.

There is another, parallel solution to our woes that should also be pursued. We acquired a sense of being in danger – and grew financially desperate – because of a failure in our relations with a few significant others. Logically, therefore, the way to recover a feeling of safety will be via our relationships, though these will be of a very different kind. Whereas the experiences and emotions that damaged us were disappointment, abandonment and emotional coldness, so what will make us feel well and safe again will be reliability, closeness, tenderness and loyalty. We must repair the damage to our psyches with the very same tool that was used to scar us.

Mansions and expensive toys have their pleasures. But what they should never be mistaken for are routes to safety and emotional ease. We should not be surprised if we remain stressed and anxious despite our wealth. Instead, we must look back to our early betrayals and find proper emotional compensation through true treasure: people who are able to love us properly.

vi.

Fear and Fame

However attractive the life of famous people may seem from afar, from close up, it is usually a very different story. Something like the following scenario is, at some stage in their career, uncommonly likely to unfold.

From the outside, all will appear to be going well. The reviews are ecstatic. The money is flowing in. The hotels are sumptuous and the private jets impeccable. The fans are eager and the dinner invitations from celebrity friends are constant. And yet, inside the mind of the famous person, there is turmoil on a scale unsuspected by almost everyone in the entourage. It started with a little niggle, but now it is a full-blown state of anxiety that begins at dawn and doesn't let up until the early hours. The famous person, beneath the smiles and the polished routines, will be contemplating the ruin of everything that they have worked for since the start. They will be imagining what might happen if a rival gets an advantage, if they make a mistake, if the critics turn against them. They will be haunted by spectres of disgrace and apprehensions of scandal. They will picture themselves having to give up the jet and take a bus. They will imagine their savings eroded and their name becoming a byword for shame.

Unable to take the panic, they might take to drink, grow intensely irritable and develop a dependence on drugs. It might seem somehow unusual and unwarranted; it is – in reality – entirely predictable.

It is extremely rare to want to be very famous without an accompanying fear of invisibility and neglect. Fame is a salve invented by the traumatised to compensate for an early experience of unbearable let-down. No one who hadn't suffered from a sense of worthlessness – one that has not been understood or worked through – would actively wish to be known by so many complete strangers.

Too often, the late-night panic of the famous results in a vow to become yet more successful and yet more well known. That, they feel, will surely quieten the fears at last. But peace of mind can never be won in this way. Ironically, however, being ever more famous just leads to more enemies, sniping, envy and the risk of scandal.

The only plausible route to safety is to become better acquainted with the original feeling of unacceptability that powered the aspiration to become exceptional – and to understand that maybe they never really wanted to be known to everyone, but rather they just wanted the love of a few very important people who (almost certainly) appeared to have better things to do or were too mentally unwell to be able to provide care.

No one ever really desires fame; they want – first and foremost – to feel loved. Fame for a time appears as though it may deliver on the original aspiration, but in reality, all it provides is paranoia and a continuous terror of downfall. The famous will truly have succeeded when they are able to walk away from being 'known' and towards the safety of being loved and seen by just one or two sets of eyes.

vii.

Impostor Syndrome

One of the most frightening eventualities that may befall us – the trigger that more than any other has the power to catapult us into dread and self-doubt – is to succeed. To be promoted, praised, given a bigger salary, told that we are brilliant and awarded great responsibility. Success has an unparalleled capacity to generate terror, a longing to confess to one's true mediocrity and a desire to run away.

Achieving little may well have its drawbacks: we feel belittled, overworked, mocked and disdained. But it spares us something far worse: having to disappoint others and be exposed as a fraud and a swindler. Inside the scared mind of the newly successful, a stream of tormenting thoughts is likely to roil: *I don't deserve this, I will be found out, I am not good enough.* In the hours ahead of a speech, all we may think of is how unworthy we are of our listeners; at a company meeting, a sense of inadequacy pursues us after every one of our utterances. We may be tempted to crash our lives deliberately, not because we relish losing what we have got, but because success has robbed us of all peace of mind.

Success is commonly held up as a universal good, but it can only satisfy us in relation to our degree of self-love. Many of us long for success but do not know how to handle it. Nothing in our past may ever have led us to expect that we might one day be widely taken for decent, honourable, talented, intelligent or likeable people. Our childhoods may have left us with the firm impression that we must, at heart, be repugnant. Perhaps, long ago, our parents forcefully conveyed the idea that nothing we did could ever be acceptable, that we were ugly and disappointing, and another sibling was always the preferred option. From this, we will have developed into people with a deep conviction of our power to revolt anyone with a close understanding of our true natures.

This is what promises to unleash a crisis the moment that success comes our way. However momentarily pleasing a promotion or a new role may be, we have no option but to conclude that those who have approved of us must have done so on the basis of a mistake – which is bound, at some point, to be identified and then corrected. Though people in the vicinity may be complimenting us, though the applause appears sincere, the error is logically about to come to light. There has been a misunderstanding on a mass scale and soon enough, we'll be accused of faking our accomplishments and defrauding our benefactors – and will face the righteous anger owed to all liars.

No wonder we can't sleep very easily. No wonder we can't stop picturing the day when we are at last unmasked. No wonder we scour social media and scan the eyes of all those we meet for the first signs of the searing revelations about to break.

So unbearable can this tension prove, we might try to assuage it by unconscious attempts to eradicate the discrepancy between the kindly verdict of the world and our private sense of low self-worth. We may start to sabotage ourselves before others get around to spotting our lies. Maybe we fluff our speech, insult our boss or leave our work undone. Before too long, to our secret relief, we will have succeeded in engineering our own downfall. We will have failed, but at least we will no longer have to be so scared of the future.

Of course, there are better, kinder ways of resolving our impostor syndrome. For a start, by accepting what our childhoods never properly taught us: that we do not need to be flawless to deserve to succeed. We can be error-prone, worried and sometimes a little silly and still not be remotely fraudulent, for this is the way every human is constituted. There is no requirement to be impeccable in all areas in order to earn the right to exist, to be loved, to be accepted and to get a raise. We don't have to hold ourselves to a standard that no one could ever reasonably be expected to meet. We must instead allow that if the world – that busy, cynical, bruised and ungenerous place – really seems to think we are good enough, then we should give ourselves the benefit of the doubt as well. Our real task is to go back and try to persuade the one audience that continues to mock us without cause: our demented inner critic, fashioned and schooled by the unrepresentative figures and experiences of early childhood.

viii.

The Benefits of a Breakdown

So dreadful can the idea of failing be in our eyes that we may spend much of our lives – and expend titanic energies – trying to avoid it. We work with ferocity, scheme relentlessly, ingratiate ourselves with people we loathe and fill every minute of the day with schemes to raise our income and highlight our name. We scan the horizon fearfully for enemies and risks. We are, in the end, engaged in an exhausting race, in which we only ever feel a few moments away from what scares us above all: the beast of failure.

For a long time, we may manage to stay just ahead of the spectre, until one day, wholly of our own accord, we come to an abrupt and surprising stop. We can't get out of bed; we can hardly speak; we can't be bothered to move or fight any more. We don't care what people are saying or what they will think. Despite everything we're meant to do and all the places we're expected to be, our deep selves are refusing to cooperate with our societal obligations. After a lifetime, something inside us can't take it any more. We're having a breakdown.

In a way, it's the very worst thing that could happen. We're about to lose all our hard-won advantages. Our boss is shocked. Friends and family may try to remain sympathetic, but the disappointment on their faces is evident; this is extremely inconvenient for everyone who depends on us. Surely we were meant to be above this sort of thing? There are panicked attempts to contact doctors and psychiatrists and hopes that some pills might quickly bring this unfortunate episode to a close. Everyone longs for normality and a return to the treadmill of success. We are a truly terrifying sight, in our pyjamas at midday, wandering around the kitchen, talking about how meaningless most of what we have ever done has really been, gazing into the middle distance at a vase of lilac flowers and mumbling how we might want to change things, and be someone else.

Breakdowns are undoubtedly frightening and a bore for those around us, but – within bounds – they can also be extremely useful. They can be occasions in which long pent-up or denied truths (about what we are angry about or deeply long for, what we want to do or who we hope to be with) punch through the veil of ordinary life and insist on being heard. A repressed authenticity fights the forces of inertia and the emotional status quo. We dare, in a way we perhaps have never done, to declare our true wishes. A breakdown may be a prelude to a breakthrough.

From our earliest years, we might have felt that if we were to gain the support of people around us, we would have to succeed on their terms rather than our own. We sensed a choice between being loved and being real and – understandably enough – chose the former. We ticked boxes of their making. We jumped through their hoops. We became practiced at precisely meeting their expectations. We put our sincere selves away and bowed to their service. We developed world-beating expertise at people-pleasing.

In our careers, we likely chose a safe but honourable profession where we could be sure of applause. We led blameless, honourable lives; we toed the line, we laughed when we needed to. We did what was expected.

But the charade could only be expected to go on for so long. At some point, a deeper and more sincere part of us realises that we are going to die soon and declares that enough is enough. If this is the price of success, we want to fail. We may be scared of poverty and disapproval, but we are now even more scared of fakery. We cannot spend the whole of our lives in hock to the demands of people we secretly despise. We want to have lived at least a little before we have to die. And so we set about smashing the edifice of prestige and respectability that we have built up. We quit our job, we tell a few false friends to go away, we sit on our own for hours looking at the sky – and we weep at how insincere and lost we have been. We tell another few friends that we have at last found our path – and they ask us how long it might be until the medication starts to work. We have wilfully brought about failure in some areas of our lives in order to allow for a deeper, slower, quieter sort of success in another.

From the prevalence of breakdowns, we can conclude that we don't simply fear failure; we also – in a strange way – long for it, because in certain incarnations, it can provide us with the energy to clear out the false gods we have been worshipping for too long. At this time, we make a resolution to stop pleasing everyone else in order to have a last, very overdue attempt at paying attention to the true self we have neglected for so long.

ix.

Fear and Paranoia

There's a certain mood which, when it takes over us, can cause us to become increasingly scared of being on the receiving end of hostility from other people: it feels as if someone may imminently want to shout at us or say mean things about us. In this state of mind, when we leave a room, we imagine that everyone inside is hating on and mocking us. We picture gossip being exchanged about us online and off. We grow afraid of enemies who may want to seize our advantages and ruin things for us. We don't necessarily have a firm grip on where the danger lies or who exactly will damage us; we simply suspect that there is something looming. In response to this eerie sensation, we may proffer, in a joking tone, that we're feeling a bit 'paranoid' at the moment – but there is nothing to laugh at. We are being slowly crippled by worry.

In an effort to reduce our apprehensions at these times, we should begin in an unusual place: with the hunch that we have problems with anger. The truth is that we are probably the sort of individual who has a great deal of difficulty confronting people who frustrate or damage them. We are unlikely to be emotionally well equipped for showdowns. We dare not speak out when others stymie our plans or bully us subtly. We might stay in relationships far longer than we should – if leaving would mean upsetting someone by whom we are privately rather intimidated. At work, we may remain endlessly stuck in unsatisfactory positions, unable to build up the courage either to quit or to fight for a promotion.

Our paranoid sensations are, arguably, the poisonous legacy of unexpressed anger. We acquire a general fear that other people will be hostile to us after having, at another time, failed to express ourselves with sufficient force and directness to a specific set of people who angered or harmed us. Paranoia is nothing more than repressed rage at other people, redirected against ourselves. It is as if a certain amount of anger is circulating in our system, seeking a way out, and when it can't find its intended target, it doesn't merely disappear, it builds up pressure and eventually ends up diverted towards the one subject who is handily close by and who won't complain: us.

Our difficulties confronting people are liable to have begun in childhood with a parent who was unable to take the slightest expression of frustration or rage. They might have been so terrifying that we never dared to raise an objection to anything they said or wanted. Instead we nodded meekly in assent to every one of their suggestions – and watched in terror as they screamed or smashed up our bedroom. Or, perhaps our caregiver appeared so fragile to us that we did our best never to contradict them; maybe they complained that we would 'be the end of them' if we caused any sort of bother. We may have heard them declaring that they would kill themselves if things got too much.

But however much we might long to smile and please (both then and now), it will be impossible not to be angry and frustrated on regular occasions. Constant meekness is only ever a front; we all have wishes that go against those of others. We all need the opportunity to make a stand. The question is where the anger goes when it can't be shown. In childhood, a rage that we can't vent in front of our parents might come back at us in the form of an intense fear that we are about to be attacked by wild animals: we have to check under the bed numerous times just to make sure that there is no pack of hyenas or pride of lions hiding there. Later on, in adulthood, the fear may emerge as a form of political paranoia, wherein anger intended for a parent takes the form of a conviction in the mendacity and nastiness of an ideology or leader. Alternatively, rage at a spouse in a cold marriage might give rise to virulent misogyny or misandry. In diverse ways, anger that is intended for someone else always comes back to damage us.

With this mechanism in mind, if we find ourselves growing ever more fearful of particular people or dynamics, rather than continuing to ruminate (or seeking to reassure ourselves about lions or politicians), we would do well to change the subject completely and ask ourselves a possibly surprising-sounding question: 'Is there anyone relatively close to home, now or in the past, with whom we are unconsciously very, very angry?'

It's probable that rather than a right- or left-wing conspiracy to 'get us', there is a parent whom we are very disappointed by. Or instead of a feminist or masculinist movement that wants to do us ill, there is a spouse we can't stand for a moment longer. Taking apart our paranoia will make the world at large feel much safer than it did, but it will also place the onus on us to do something we have resisted for too long: realise that we have the right to complain, that other people won't be able to harm us if we do and that we should dare to speak – with courage and politeness – lest meekness ends up destroying us.

X.

On Not Thinking Straight

It would be reassuring to believe that our degree of intelligence is relatively impervious to our emotional state; that, broadly speaking, we remain as clever as we ever are whatever happens to be unfolding for us emotionally. Of course, in certain very dramatic moments, it's expected that our cleverness might take a hit: it would be hard to do quadratic equations accurately if there was a tiger in the room. But on the whole, surely one or two waves of emotional disturbance shouldn't knock out a faculty as central and as long-established as intelligence ...

This, however, is to underestimate the extent to which – awkwardly – our powers of reason are apt to fail us entirely under particular conditions. By all objective measures we may display every sign of high intelligence: we may have an excellent grasp of history and politics, science and art. We may be capable of running a sizeable team or managing a high-profile career. And yet, faced with certain challenges, we are wont to relapse into the reasoning patterns of the very young and very unqualified child we once were.

It appears by the way our minds are built, that no age that we have ever travelled through is ever entirely superseded and rendered inaccessible to us. Like a Russian doll, beneath an adult shell we contain all our past selves, to which we will be sent back according to outer circumstances. A person who was bullied by an overbearing parent as a 5-year-old may, since then, have acquired two PhDs, gained membership in an elite intellectual circle and have raised a family. And yet when this unfortunate soul comes up against a bullying older adversary, they may have no capacity whatsoever to approach them as an adult with a right to live – let alone a deep understanding of Roman law, the novels of George Eliot and the workings of semiconductors. Instead, they meet this parental figure once again as a shy and defenceless child, worried that they are going to be hit or annihilated, and as a result, they struggle to form coherent sentences or remember their own name. We are apt to return to precisely the degree of intelligence that we possessed when certain difficulties arose in childhood and seared themselves across our neuronal pathways. Trauma keeps us as cognitively limited as we were when a given disaster struck us.

The way in which our intelligence is hampered by our emotions means that we misread reality without noticing our blindness. For example, we might be unable to recognise that someone is treating us unfairly in an intimate relationship and that we would have every right to make a complaint, because we grew up to expect this kind of treatment and to not question it. Our sizeable intelligence walks right past an issue that would immediately attract the attention of any moderately interested outsider.

Or we may be unable to consider the extent of our freedom and our options to leave a job or start a new life, because our intelligence has been silenced by an emotional expectation that suffering and resignation are our dues. We may also find it impossible to see that we are falling into depression because a chance to be angry was never granted to us, or that we are developing a paranoia as an alternative to directing anger back at an adversary, or that we are impelled to crash our career because of an impression of unworthiness.

Fear isn't only unpleasant – it makes us 'stupid'. Yet, devilishly, it does so in ways that we can't easily observe. Our reasoning faculties switch off, but without granting us even a hint that they are doing so. We don't sense our panic; we don't feel our intellectual wattage being dialled down to close to zero. We have no subjective awareness of when our adult brains are quietly unplugged and surreptitiously replaced by those of naïve and terrified infants.

Even if we cannot grasp that we are not thinking straight – and perhaps because of that fact – we should allow for the overall possibility of the phenomenon and make the necessary adjustments. We should forgive our traumatised minds for not being able to yield an accurate picture of the world, its threats and its options, and treat them with good humour. We shouldn't feel insulted that, without warning, we will at times be as cognitively limited as a worried, shamed and naïve

4-year-old. In turn, when we find ourselves in emotional zones that we identify as dangerous, we should take care to have a few other adequately sized brains around us into which, like a machine with a depleted battery, we can plug ourselves – so as to recalibrate our assessment of the choices in front of us.

At moments when we are convinced that failure is staring us in the face, when we are sure that bankruptcy, abandonment, exile or disgrace is about to strike, we should do ourselves the favour of imagining that we are, perhaps, not in any danger at all; rather we have stopped being able to think straight. We have done so not because we are inherently stupid (it would be easier if we were), but because while we are extremely intelligent, at this instant – due to an invisible and regrettable connection between our present-day challenge and one in the past that we had to face without adequate love or care – we have regressed to an earlier state of cognitive ability and most of our brain is not available for use.

Rather than continuing to take our fears as facts, we should good-naturedly accept that our minds are simply prone to faulty readings; that there almost certainly is no tiger in the room, no monster about to swallow us and no catastrophe about to destroy everything. There is simply an adult mind that, for very good and very sad reasons, has completely stopped working for a while – and needs some help.

xi.

Self-compassion

The more we start to understand the origins of our fearful worldview, the more we may decide that we have the right to do something which we have perhaps indulged in very little over the years: feel sorry for ourselves.

By their nature, our characters are likely to resist the temptation to take our side. We may feel that we're not the sort to weep over our fate or feel that we have been given a particularly bad set of cards. And yet, the more we revisit the past and consequently get a handle on the causes of our fears, the more we may allow ourselves one or two moments of compassion for the experiences we've been exposed to and their repercussions down the decades. We have grown into fear-laden people because, when we were far too young to interpret and manage what was happening, we were let down. Someone shouted at us inordinately and didn't allow us to get annoyed back. Someone told us that we would only ever be acceptable if we achieved extraordinary things. Someone gave us the impression that we didn't deserve to succeed. Someone didn't come to soothe us when we were screaming in the night and was unable to equip us with the tools to dampen our panic and sorrows in adult life. These people may not have intended to cause harm, but we have been severely wounded nevertheless.

In the broadest sense, we are afraid of failure because we were not properly loved. We were not held, reassured, calmed down, delighted in and accepted unconditionally. We believe that the world is filled with risks, not because we face unprecedented obstacles, but because we have unusually difficult histories. The catastrophe we apprehend has in fact already happened, but until now we have found it too hard to think about it. We were too busy working, trying to impress or fending off imagined enemies.

But now, in a quiet corner of our minds, we can finally take the chance to behave like a loving parent towards our frightened and frantic inner self. We can sit ourselves on our own knee, stroke our own forehead, hold our own hand and tell ourselves that we are – whatever we may think – a very interesting and kindly person whom it is a privilege to know and to look after. We can congratulate ourselves on how hard we have tried and what enormous efforts we have made. We can tell ourselves that perhaps now is a time for change – that there has been enough endless material and status striving, enough jockeying for position and hope for preferment, enough busyness and exhaustion, self-flagellation and masochism. Now, instead, there is a chance to reorient our lives towards greater relational warmth. We can whisper, away from the sarcastic and brutal alternative voices who still like to shout inside us, that the time for fear has come to an end – and that a reign of love and safety can begin.

xii.

A Less Pressured Life

As anxious, easily frightened people, we are likely to miss a crucial detail in the path to a calmer life: that is, that we cannot find calm simply on the basis of taking in a few ideas. In order to construct the quieter, less pressured lives we long for – lives in which we might be able to minimise contact with the sorts of events, people and opinions that torment and sadden us – we need also to alter our habits.

What might some of the elements of a less pressured existence look like?

Naps

Kindly parents in charge of young children know full well the dangers of exhaustion: how quickly it can descend, how unaware one can be that it has and how terrible everything looks under its governance. A parent's first thought, whenever there is a tantrum or hysteria, is whether it might be time to go upstairs, close the curtains and lie down for forty minutes. They will refuse to engage in a discussion about sweets or toys or trips, not because these aren't legitimate topics, but because they know that so long as the mind has not rested, no good conclusions can ever be reached.

Wise adults should consider themselves as identical to 9-month-olds in this sense. We should not be interested in marathons of endurance. Rather, as soon as we notice our panic rising and latching on viciously to an ever-expanding array of topics, we must recognise what is going to happen – and know better than to try to think our way out of fear with only an exhausted brain for assistance. The wise adult is sufficiently committed to serenity to have a proper reverence for beds.

Processing time

The anxious-yet-wise also know to allow plenty of time in which to 'process' experiences. That is, to sift through what has happened in order to put it into perspective, tease out any worrying elements, return ideas to more reasonable forms and plan a way out of any dreaded eventualities. To do this we must sit in a comfortable place, in an armchair or by the window, probably with a pen and paper, and go through what has gone on, occasionally jotting something down, circling a word or connecting sentences with arrows. We should tend to matters like skilful gardeners, removing new shoots of worry and raking the weeds of our minds. The wise adult knows that enough goes on in an average day of an active life to fill half an hour or more of processing time – and that insomnia and stretches of panic are likely to be our minds' revenge for the thoughts we have carefully managed not to have when we are 'busy'. As enlightened souls, we will be hard-working enough to allow ourselves plenty of time to 'do nothing' – other than reflect and recollect.

Media

Keeping a screen permanently to hand that can inform us of every latest piece of nastiness, folly, envy and anger at large in the world poses an existential threat to the mind – and is a fast route to madness for anyone of fragile disposition. We are far too delicately constituted to be able to blithely read salacious accounts of yet more murders, divorces or business failures – and then hope to get on with our day with our spirits remotely intact. If we are to remain even somewhat balanced, limiting our contact with, and knowledge of, the actions and beliefs of most members of the human race will be a daily priority.

Clouds, streams, trees

To lay claim to the steadiness and objectivity we need, we would be well advised to spend as much time as possible contemplating phenomena wholly disconnected from our immediate concerns. We should be sure to take a lot of walks outside.

On the way, we should look up. Clouds, thankfully, know nothing of us – they float by utterly unaware of our concerns. We can be reminded that everything will pass, even the current nastiness and anxiety, just as the clouds that seemed so fixed and heavy but an hour ago have now moved on, leaving behind only two or three of their number, apologetic and timid before the victorious sun.

We should look at trees, those role models of patience and resolution. Their gnarled, worn barks speak of the hundreds of seasons they have endured. They have bent and lost branches in winter winds, they have been gnawed at by worms and beetles across the airless days of summer, they have been knocked and hacked at by farmers and children. But they endure – as we might better learn to do through their example.

We should contemplate streams. Their constant activity enlivens the imagination. They don't stare blankly back at us, like pieces of paper on a desk. They distract our minds just enough that the good ideas – the ones that we are hesitant to ask ourselves directly – can feel relieved of pressure and slip out.

We need nature not just for physical health, but, just as importantly, for relief from the tensions of our psyches. No day should be counted as wise if it does not include at least a few moments given over to clouds, trees or streams: robust emissaries of perspective, patience and introspection.

Friends

We cannot afford to keep surrounding ourselves with those witty, popular, sometimes-interesting types whom we nevertheless know – deep down – would run away at the first sign of trouble. We can't have amusing-but-treacherous friends when our mental well-being is in question. We need allies, however anonymous and outwardly unimpressive they might be, who would offer to spring us out of prison if required. There is no point befriending anyone who cannot understand and tolerate our pain.

Voluntary retirement

In our pursuit of serenity, we should understand the connection between money, power and renown on the one hand, and our reserves of calm on the other. We must not imagine that we can ever add more of the former without decreasing the latter. We can certainly design a life where we fill our coffers, are recognised by strangers and are invited to seemingly important occasions – but we must recognise that we will also, by necessity, be increasing the amount of panic and paranoia in our lives. We should dare to retire voluntarily from an active or elite life – in order to enjoy the true wealth afforded by a serene mind.

xiii.

Thinking of the Worst

When we are worried about failure and take our anxieties to our friends, the response that we are most likely to receive is that our fears are overblown and will almost certainly never come to pass. The error won't be uncovered, the slip-up wasn't noticed, the enemy isn't so nasty, people won't mind; *it will be fine*.

At first it sounds almost entirely reassuring. But something within the optimism being offered is likely to leave us with an uneasy feeling – one that we can't entirely shake off, and that has a habit of reappearing late at night or when we are in a jittery mood. We desperately want to believe that we are safe, but what if – after all, despite the reassurance – we are not? Are there not many cases in which, despite good odds, things nevertheless go very, very wrong?

What if the error *is* uncovered, what if our mistake *is* treated harshly – what if the world ends up in an unforgiving frame of mind?

These questions can pursue us relentlessly, growing ever more impervious to our optimism. We may try to pile more reassurance onto the fire of worry, but no matter what we attempt, the anxiety continues to mount. It's at this point that we should try an initially alarming, but ultimately profoundly fruitful, move: *thinking about, and making friends with, the very worst.*

Rather than assuming that we will be saved, we should deliberately try to imagine every fear turning into reality: the shock of our clients, the surprise of our colleagues, the scandalised headlines in newspapers, the arrival of the police, the jeering of crowds, the packed courtroom, the bare prison cell, the lost decade in an institution, the desertion of lovers, the contempt of one's children, the ruin of every last hope.

It might sound like a recipe for cataclysmic panic, but far from it: careful, close-up, reasoned examination of the worst-case scenario is liable to throw up a surprising fact: that the worst is actually survivable. Desirable it certainly isn't, awful it would often be, but it would also – overall – turn out to be something that we could, just, get through.

We could – when we think about it – imagine losing all but two good friends and surviving. We could imagine spending a few years in prison or becoming a byword for infamy – and surviving. It absolutely wouldn't be what we would wish for, but, all things considered, it would be endurable.

What our minds are especially and unduly tortured by is uncertainty. Often, what worries us most are outcomes that we cannot divine, issues over which we lack any firm control or definitive information: we can't foresee whether we'll get the right grades in an exam, we can't know whether a business will go bust, we have no total assurance \ about whether our relationship will survive.

In such a situation, hungry for certainty, the racing, anxious mind throws us into constant turmoil. Wishing to be reassured completely, it keeps us awake with a litany of the same familiar questions: *Will we be OK? Will the bad thing happen? Is it going to be fine?*

To close off this tortuous cycle of never-ending questions, we should boldly stand up to our nagging selves and deliver a very definitive-sounding answer. We must assume that everything terrible will happen, and then concentrate all our energy on trying to figure out how the terrible might turn out to be bearable – which it will be, for certain.

It's an ineradicable part of being human that we simply cannot know what elements of suffering we will need to pass through before we are at last delivered to our final resting place. Every day sees us walk – usually blithely – past a thousand risks. We may continue to pass through unharmed – or else a blunder or two will wind us up in infamy, poverty and shame. Right now, in another part of town or a faraway continent, our sad end may be being worked out. Disaster might strike by nightfall. We don't need any formal belief in the gods to appreciate that our destinies are not in our own hands; that at any moment (whatever our levels of wealth, probity, youth or vigour) we might fall prey to the most appalling reversals – and so we would be wise to walk lightly and with reverence across the unpredictable, troubled face of the Earth.

Nevertheless, we can buttress our natural exposure to fate with a tenacious degree of defiant stoic pessimism. We don't have to greet the unknown in terror, on our knees, quivering. We may stand up tall, knowing that the most egregious events might visit us, but that we would – somehow – find a way through them. And, if we couldn't, if every single breath was agony, we might even darkly allow – despite a million careful caveats – that the pain wouldn't have to be endless. It's in the context of the reassuring power of the very darkest thoughts that we can approach failure.

Many of us will never have to face real-world failure, but we will be haunted and tortured by the idea that we might have to – and in no position to be comforted by easy suggestions that things are sure to be fine. This is why we must consider at length the practical and psychological realities of extreme failure (the ideal sort of hut to build and how to handle the desertion of all our friends). Not because we will fail, but because the only way to dilute our fears is to examine the thought that we might in exhaustive detail – and thereby realise that it can be borne.

Those afraid of failure and those who have failed have much to offer one another. The failed are living proof that failure can be endured – while the fearful are an ideal constituency on which the failed (especially if they are looking out for new employment that can grant them a gainful sense of service) can practise their wisdom and deliver solace.

We waste far too much time scaling or dreaming of the peaks of worldly success. Now is the moment to turn our attention to becoming those unlikely, but much more important, members of society: good failures. These are people who know how to be kind, empathetic, gentle, humorous, humble, grateful and imaginative in the face of disaster – and who are therefore always ready to lend a hand to fellow vulnerable, ailing humans who have been damned by fate and who, for now, struggle to remember any reasons to live. That will be redemption and success properly worthy of the word.

Picture Credits

Cover   Mathias P.R. Reding / Unsplash

p. 18   Pieter Bruegel the Elder, *The Triumph of Death*, c. 1562–1563. Oil on panel, 117 cm × 162 cm. Museo del Prado, Madrid, Spain / Wikimedia Commons

p. 87t   Courtesy of Czerny's International Auction House

p. 87b   Illustration from an 18th-century chapbook. Reproduced in John Ashton, *Chapbooks of the Eighteenth Century*, 1834 / Wikimedia Commons

p. 89t   © Stiftung Stadtmuseum Berlin

p. 89b   Rosser1954 / Wikimedia Commons

p. 103   Clemens Bewer, *Johann Wilhelm Janssen and his Family*, 1843. 125 cm × 155 cm. Couven Museum, Aachen, Germany

p. 105   Octave Tassaert, *Studio Interior*, 1845. Oil on canvas, 46 cm × 38 cm. Louvre Museum, Paris, France / Wikimedia Commons

p. 124   John Profumo with the Social Care and Leisure Centre minibus, 1998. Image from the Toynbee Hall collection (reference: LMA/4683/IMG/01/10/003/142)

p. 129t   Xiang Shengmo, *Reading in the Autumn Forest*, 1623. Ink and colour on paper, 106.5 cm × 34.5 cm. The British Museum, London © The Trustees of the British Museum

p. 129b   Tang Yin, *Thatched Cottage in the Western Mountains*, c. 1499–1520. Ink and colour on paper, 31.2 cm × 146.3 cm. The British Museum, London © The Trustees of the British Museum

p. 145   Florilegius / Alamy Stock Photo

The School of Life is a global organisation helping people lead more fulfilled lives. It is a resource for helping us understand ourselves, for improving our relationships, our careers and our social lives – as well as for helping us find calm and get more out of our leisure hours. We do this through films, workshops, books, apps, gifts and community. You can find us online, in stores and in welcoming spaces around the globe.